INTO THE LIGHT

INTO THE LIGHT

A Complete History of Sunderland Football Club

Roger Hutchinson

MAINSTREAM
PUBLISHING

EDINBURGH AND LONDON

First published in Great Britain in 1999 by
MAINSTREAM PUBLISHING COMPANY (EDINBURGH) LTD
7 Albany Street
Edinburgh EH1 3UG

ISBN 1 84018 216 4

A catalogue record for this book is available from the British Library

Typeset in Berkeley Book
Printed and bound in Great Britain by Creative Print Design

Contents

Preface

Sunday, 10 October 1999 was a significant day in the north-east of England. At the Stadium of Light on Wearside the English national football team was playing one of its few matches away from Wembley. It was – as things turned out – an optimistic occasion. Twenty-four hours earlier Sweden had beaten Poland, thereby throwing England a lifeline to qualify via play-offs for the 2000 European Championships. The question on many people's minds was: would England's players throw it back again? The nation's first opportunity to judge came that Sunday afternoon at the ground of Sunderland AFC. It was the first time that England had played in Sunderland since November 1950, when goals from Baily, Mannion and a certain Jackie Milburn beat Wales by 4–2.

Not many features had survived the 49 years between those two fixtures. They did not even take place on the same ground. Sunderland had by October 1999 moved from Roker Park, their famous twentieth-century home, to the brand spanking new Stadium of Light. And England, it might be said, had themselves gone down rather in the rankings of international soccer.

But one or two similarities remained. Both games took place before a large and raucous crowd. Both games took place at the ground of a football club which was not only at the top of the premier division in English football, but which expected to stay there. Both England teams contained a Sunderland player, the freescoring Kevin Phillips having been called up by international manager Kevin Keegan to repeat his club form on home soil. And both England teams contained a superb attacking footballer who came from the north-east, who scored on that and on many other occasions – but who happened to be on the books of Newcastle United.

All the same, the Stadium of Light rose to salute Alan Shearer's goal for England against Belgium, as 49 years earlier Roker Park had roared its appreciation of Jackie Milburn's strike against Wales. Neither occasions signalled any more than a slight lull in hostilities; a temporary ceasefire. But they were nice to see.

Truly great football clubs and their supporters define themselves less by reference to their rivals, and more by their own achievements. When in the last ten years of the nineteenth century and the first decade of the twentieth, Sunderland and Newcastle United were swapping dominance of the national game like a couple of relay runners, handing on titles and cups to each other, the north-east was incomparably the heart and the head of English football. Their rivalry helped. In the season 1999–2000, once again those two great clubs (and Middlesbrough) are together in the top tier of the game. When the Stadium of Light hosted that England international, Sunderland were in fact close to the top of the Premiership and looking capable of mounting a serious challenge for the title, or at least for a prominent European place.

A confidence accrues in any region as the result of such success. You do not need to write the history of such an institution as Sunderland AFC to see what the club has brought to Wearside, in good economic times and in bad. It has celebrated the success of the late-Victorian era, and it has helped massively to ease the difficulties of the depression years in that part of the country.

Clubs like that are more than sporting organisations. They are part of the definition of a city, of a region. The great name of Sunderland was for many years resident in its football team. As it enters its third century, restored once again to its rightful place on top of the English game, in a ground fit to host international matches, with a team and a manager comparable not only to the best of their time, but also (and this is the harsher comparison) to the best in their club's astonishing history . . . well, the season ticket holders are fortunate. And not just because they get to see, for the first time in 49 years, England games.

Roger Hutchinson
Isle of Raasay, 1999

ONE

The Team Of All The Talents

September 1890

The eleven footballers who walked onto the turf of Sunderland AFC's Newcastle Road ground on 13 September 1890 were wearing the buttoned-up shirts of scarlet and white stripes and the knee-length navy-blue trousers, which had four years earlier replaced the team's original colours of blue shirts and pants. Newcastle Road was packed. An 'immense throng of spectators' – unspecified in the records, but certainly over 10,000, and probably approaching the ground capacity of 15,000 – had gathered to watch Sunderland's first game in the Football League.

They, players and fans alike, had reason for optimism. Sunderland AFC were, after all, older than the Football League itself. September 1890 saw the beginning of the league's third season as a 12-club single-division competition based entirely in the midlands and the north of England. Since their own foundation 11 years earlier Sunderland had competed without much success in the venerable old FA Cup, but their record in friendly matches was excellent.

In the previous season they had played no fewer than 47 games, winning 34, drawing four and losing nine – and scoring in the process an extraordinary 155 goals. Six of those victories, three of those draws and only four of those defeats had been against established Football League clubs. Middle-of-the-table Accrington had been despatched 8–2. And the league runners-up of the year before, Aston Villa, had been memorably spanked by 7–2. This thrashing led the Villa official and founder of the Football League, William MacGregor, to utter the famous line: 'They [Sunderland] have a talented man in every position.'

So the Team Of All The Talents[1] entered the Football League that September afternoon with no little confidence. On the previous Saturday, in a pre-season warm-up friendly, Sunderland had faced the holders of the league championship for the last two (and first two) seasons. Preston North End had gone home at the wrong end of a 6–3 hiding. And the first opponents to visit Newcastle Road in a Football League match were Burnley FC, who had finished fourth from bottom and second-bottom respectively in the first two league seasons.

The Team Of All The Talents could, by 13 September 1890, have been equally accurately described as the Side Of All The Scots. Only three of the eleven players had been born south of the border, and one of those three had been signed from a Scottish club.

Six of the nine Scottish-based players had been brought to Wearside in the previous year. The reason was simple. Professional soccer – the paying of wages to footballers and officials alike – had been legalised in England in 1885. It would stay illegal in Scotland until 1893. In order to make a living from the game, the talented and progressive Scottish players of the day had to travel south. They did so in droves, naturally preferring the professional English clubs closest to their homeland – Sunderland, and later Newcastle United. In 1889 and 1890, as they prepared for the Football League, Sunderland AFC had the pick of a large and ambitious pool of Caledonian brilliance.

In that September league début match only the Sunderland goalkeeper and two full-backs were English. This may not have been purely coincidental. Between 1867 and 1925 the offside rule

---

[1] This phrase resonated across the land in the early 1890s and is still recalled to this day. It certainly originated in late-Victorian recollection of the short-lived Tory coalition government, the 'Ministry of all the Talents' of 1806–07.

insisted that an attacking forward should have *three* opposing players between himself and the goal when a pass was played to him. These were usually, of course, the goalkeeper and two full-backs. Sunderland's manager Tom Watson may have considered that a national unity of purpose and a shared English dialect between his back three would be helpful in co-ordinating such tactics.

The goalkeeper was a local man, Bill 'Stonewall' Kirtley, who had been on the club's books since 1885. The right-back, 'Dowk' Oliver, was another Wearsider from Castletown, whom Sunderland had signed from Southwick FC in 1887. The left-back, Tom Porteous, was the Englishman who had been playing as an amateur for Kilmarnock in Scotland before signing professional terms with Sunderland in 1889. Porteous would become the first Sunderland player to be capped by England when he was picked to play against Wales in 1891.

And then came the Scots: all eight of them, comprising the entire half-back and forward lines. They were led by the captain and centre-half, John Robertson Auld. The 22-year-old Johnny Auld had three Scottish caps and a Scottish Cup-winners' medal hanging from his belt when he arrived in the north-east of England from Third Lanark in 1889.

The terms of Auld's arrival at Newcastle Road give us an insight into the finances of the English professional game in 1889 and 1890. He received a signing-on fee of £150 (about £8,000 at the end of the twentieth century); another £20 (£1,100) for signing professional forms; and £50 (£2,700) towards rental on a boot and shoe shop in Sunderland's Union Street, which the club also fitted out. On top of this Auld was paid £300 (£16,000) as two years' wages in advance. The standard weekly wage for Sunderland's first-team professionals in the Football League was soon fixed at Auld's level – £3 (£160) a week, although very few of them received the new captain's signing-on benefits.

Auld was flanked on his right by Hugh Wilson from New Milnes in Ayrshire. Wilson also arrived in the autumn of 1889 with a Scottish cap. He was to win two more while signed for Sunderland – at a time when the Scottish FA was reluctant to field 'Anglos' for the national side, considering them unprincipled mercenaries – and another, remarkably, as late as 1904, when Wilson was back in Scotland playing for Third Lanark. Wilson, who would replace Auld as Sunderland's captain, was noted for his unusually effective running throw-ins. They were not, as legend has it, one-handed throws – players had been obliged to take throw-ins with both hands since 1882. But until 1895 a throw could be taken from anywhere, at a gallop, and without both feet on the ground. Hughie Wilson's dramatic throws were known to reach the middle of the six-yard box, and helped to prompt the rule-change by the spoil-sport Football Association five years after his league début.

Completing the half-back line on Auld's left was Willie Gibson, who had arrived from Cambuslang in the August of 1888. Gibson was tempted back to Glasgow to play for his beloved Rangers at the start of the Scottish professional era in 1894, but returned after a season to Sunderland.

Those three half-backs were ordinarily fronted by a five-man forward-line based upon the 'Renton charge' – three formidable footballers, all signed in 1889 from the top Scottish club Renton FC. They were the outside-right, little John Harvie; the deadly goalscoring international John Campbell at centre-forward; and the inside-left/left-winger David Hannah. In between the Renton charge were another Scottish cap at inside-right, Jimmy Miller, who had also arrived in 1889 from Annbank; and at inside-left the Coatbridge man Jack Scott, who signed from Albion Rovers in June 1890. The three Renton players must have been particularly pleased to be on Wearside as the 1890–91 season developed. Back home, their old club had been chiefly responsible for launching a Scottish League in that year. After just five league games, however, Renton FC was accused by the Scottish FA of playing a friendly against Edinburgh St Bernard's, a renegade squad which was suspected of paying its footballers. Renton were consequently banned from the remainder of the first season of the competition which they had created.

With minor changes, that forward line would serve Sunderland well for several remarkable seasons. Just before the first big kick-off against Burnley on 13 September 1890, however, John Harvie had to call off. The reserve right-winger, another Scot called John Spence, who had signed from Kilmarnock late in 1889, was drafted into Harvie's place at the last minute. (We do not know the reason, but the fact that Harvie's name was actually listed on the team-sheet suggests a late injury or minor illness.) If there was a weak link in the Team Of All The Talents, mused the huge Wearside crowd, it could only be Spence. But things did not turn out that way.

John Campbell kicked off under a scorching sun at 3.16 p.m., and from the very start Burnley looked superior. Their two seasons of league competition had clearly given them an edge in competent defending. They comfortably contained Sunderland's early excited push, before launching a couple of dangerous counter-attacks which Porteous struggled to clear. And then suddenly, shockingly, Burnley were 1–0 ahead: a three-man move resulting in a shot high over Kirtley into the net.

Sunderland responded ferociously, winning corner after corner but failing to break down the visitors' defence until a long ball from Gibson set Campbell free, and the centre-forward squared for Spence to score the first goal by a Sunderland player in the Football League. Having equalised before a delirious crowd, Sunderland found themselves pressed back once more by Burnley. Campbell was penalised for a foul in the penalty area, directly in front of Kirtley's goals – but the penalty kick was not yet part of soccer (it would not be introduced until the following year). Referee Fitzroy Norris from Bolton could only give a free-kick to Burnley, and that was cleared by Oliver.

Auld, Campbell and Spence forced another corner; and then it was Sunderland's turn to squander a free-kick in the opposition's box. Then, in quick succession, Spence shot wide, shot into goal but was disallowed for offside – and just 60 seconds later the Scot grabbed his second to put Sunderland 2–1 ahead. The crowd's joy was short-lived. Before half-time Burnley equalised, and then took a 3–2 lead. After the break, all the visitors needed to do was keep Sunderland at bay to take the two points back to Lancashire, and in the face of increasingly desperate Sunderland pressure, they achieved it.

Two days later, on the afternoon of Monday, 15 September, Sunderland played their second league fixture – also at home – to Wolverhampton Wanderers. Harvie was available, and picked on the right wing, but the two-goal Spence was retained in the first team, taking Gibson's place at left-half. One other change was made, and it would prove significant in the years to come. James Gillespie, yet another Scottish international forward who had arrived in the previous year from Renton, replaced Jimmy Miller at inside-right.

A reduced weekday crowd of 5,000 paying fans saw an extraordinary spectacle. Gillespie, Campbell and Scott gave the Wearsiders what should have been an impregnable 3–0 lead by half-time. But Wolves hit back in the second half with such ferocity that they caught and overhauled the home side, finishing as 4–3 winners.

The poor goalkeeper, who had not been well, took the blame. After five seasons of friendlies and Durham Cup finals and FA Cup matches, 'Stonewall' Kirtley had played his last match for Sunderland AFC. He was kept on the books as a reserve until 1892, when he was transferred to the doomed poor relations, non-league Sunderland Albion. Manager Watson had five days in which to act before his third league match, away to West Bromwich Albion.

Watson wasted no time, and he looked in a familiar direction. The 22-year-old Scottish international goalkeeper John Edward 'Ned' Doig had fallen out with his club, Arbroath. Doig had turned out for Blackburn Rovers in a friendly match, and as a result of that flirtation with English professionalism Arbroath had suspended their custodian. The aggrieved Doig responded happily to Watson's approach, signed for Sunderland in midweek, and played against West Brom on Saturday, 20 September.

In the long term, it was an inspirational signing. Ned – or 'Teddy', as he became known on Wearside – Doig would dominate the Sunderland goals for a further 14 seasons. But in the short term it was almost disastrous. Doig kept a clean sheet at West Brom, and the returning Miller collected two goals, which alongside Campbell and Scott's single strikes gave Sunderland an impressive 4–0 away win. But Sunderland, in their haste to bolster their last line of defence and their unfamiliarity with the ways of the Football League, failed to get Doig's registration form in on time. They were fined £25 and – more crucially – they were also docked two points, their first two points in the league.

After three matches the Team Of All The Talents sat at the bottom of the Football League, with precisely no points. Only a soothsayer – or, perhaps, William MacGregor of Aston Villa – could have predicted what would happen next . . . The astounding run of form which took these newcomers to within six points (those vital six points!) of the league championship, and to the semi-finals of the FA Cup; the subsequent three league championships in four seasons; the total of five championships, three runners-up slots, three FA Cup semi-finals and one FA Cup final, all in the few short years before the First World War suspended play . . . Nobody, not even the extraordinary Tom Watson, could have predicted that.

TWO

The Dawn of the 'Scottish Craze'

1879–1891

Fittingly enough, it was all started by a Scot.

James Allan arrived straight from Glasgow University to teach in Sunderland in 1877. To his disappointment, the association code of football – which was achieving great popularity in his native Scotland – was played hardly at all in the north-east of England, where rugby was the predominant winter team sport. Allan uncovered a group of other teachers in the area who shared his interest in righting this wrong, and at a meeting in Norfolk Street in the October of 1879 the Sunderland and District Teachers' Association Football Club was formed.

It was an amateur club. In those early days the Football Association had made no ruling for or against professionalism. It had no need to do so, as most clubs were amateur from necessity. Soccer was not yet a mass spectator sport. But the amateurism of the Sunderland Teachers' Club was its undoing. The men rented a ground at Hendon for £10 a year (equivalent to £600 or so, 120 years later – but although the amount may not seem staggering, teachers' wages were insubstantial in 1879) and by the end of a single season they found it difficult to pay the rent and travelling costs to meet their few opponents, scattered across the north-east.

And so in October 1880 they called a meeting which discussed two options: to close the club, or to open it to non-teaching members. They agreed upon the latter, and Sunderland and District Teachers' Association Football Club became simply Sunderland Association Football Club.

The new club promptly entered for the Northumberland & Durham Challenge Cup, drew a bye in the first round, and began to arrange competitive friendlies. In the first, they were beaten 1–0 by Ferryhill. Two weeks later, on 27 November 1880, James Allan scored twice in a 4–0 friendly defeat of Ovingham. In the middle of December two more Allan goals saw them dismiss Burnopfield from the second round of the Northumberland & Durham Cup; and in February 1881 they travelled to a venue on the outskirts of Newcastle named St James's Park, where they were knocked out of the cup by a side called Newcastle Rangers.

For the next couple of seasons James Allan – who looks increasingly like that commonplace figure in association football, the man who starts a team to showcase his own talents – kept knocking in the goals, but despite one appearance in the 1883 final Sunderland never won the Northumberland & Durham Cup. Only after the collapse of the Northumberland & Durham Association and the subsequent foundation of the Durham FA, and of the Durham Cup, did the young club seize its first silverware.

On 5 April 1884 Darlington travelled to the 'neutral' arena of the old cricket ground on Newcastle Road to meet Sunderland in the first final of the Durham Cup. Sunderland won comfortably, by 4–0. But the game had aroused an unexpected – if promising – level of local interest. As many as 2,000 fans crowded the touch-line, and by the end of the game things seemed to be getting out of hand. It is inevitable that such numbers will have spilt onto the pitch at regular intervals, possibly interfering with play occasionally. According to Darlington FC, who lodged an immediate protest, they certainly intimidated both the Whitburn referee and the visiting players.

The Durham FA upheld Darlington's protest, 'after heated discussion', and ordered the final to be replayed at Birtley on 3 May. The DFA also took the extraordinary step of inviting the current president of football's founding body, the 21-year-old English Football Association, to referee the replay. Major Francis Marindin agreed, and this time Sunderland, in their all-blue shirts and knickerbockers, beat Darlington by just 2–0.

The club's founder James Allan failed to score in either the first or the replayed Durham Cup final, which – given his extraordinary scoring record in other games – suggests that he was not playing. If so, he soon got a form of compensation. Allan was one of six Sunderland players selected for the Durham County select side which played Northumberland in 1884. (Allan was outside-right. The others were the inside-left J. MacDonald, who scored in both cup finals; the entire half-back line of Buchanan, Hindle and MacMillan; and the goalkeeper Green.) And on 20 December 1884 Allan set a record which will probably never be beaten. Castletown visited Sunderland for what was supposed to be a Durham Cup first round tie. But as the visitors arrived with just eight men the cup tie was called off. Sunderland lent them three reserves and a friendly was played which the home team won by 23–0. Of Sunderland's record total, James Allan – an entertaining footballer who could be 'pleasantly clownish' – contributed no fewer than 12 goals.

At the start of the 1884–85 season Sunderland had moved to a new ground, the pitch used by St Bede's FC at Abbs Field, Fulwell. The significance of this was that Abbs Field was enclosed, and so Sunderland AFC could begin to charge an entrance fee – proof in itself of the growing popularity of soccer as a spectator sport on Wearside.

It was an eventful season. In 1884–85 Sunderland entered the FA Cup for the first time, going down 3–1 at Redcar in the zoned first round; entertained their first Scottish 'friendly' visitors (Port Glasgow, who emphasised the difference in class north of the border by winning 11–0); signed their first two Scottish players, A. White and J. Hunter, both from Kilmarnock; and reached the final of the Durham Cup for the second consecutive year, once more facing Darlington (who took their revenge, and the cup back south, by winning 3–0).

A month after that final, on 25 April 1885, the local man William Kirtley made his début for Sunderland. 'Stonewall' Kirtley would be the club's first-choice goalkeeper for a further six years, until that sad afternoon at home to Wolves in Sunderland's second Football League game. Two years after that incident in 1890, in the September of 1892 Kirtley was transferred from Sunderland reserves. But he only went as far as Sunderland Albion, and 'Stonewall' would eventually return to the club which he had done so much to establish. In the middle of the 1930s the old man looking after Sunderland AFC's billiard table at the famous Roker Park ground was none other than the team's first regular first-team goalkeeper – the local boy who had stood between the posts in their first Football League match.

We can recognise, then, some of the names on the team-sheet for the next FA Cup first round tie on 24 October 1885 – once more against Redcar, once more away. There was Kirtley in goals. There was Hunter from Kilmarnock at left-back (White had quickly returned to Scotland). There was MacMillan, the Durham Select player and Sunderland captain, at right-half. And there were the goalscorers MacDonald and Allan, at centre-forward and inside-left respectively.

They failed once more, losing 3–0. But there remain, from that cup tie in another century, the match-day finances of Sunderland AFC. It cost the club £6 1s 8½d to travel to Redcar, and their share of the gate was £5 11s 5d. It was presumably a small gate, and Sunderland could expect at least to break even from attractive fixtures at Abbs Field. Indeed, when Port Glasgow returned for another friendly on 1 January 1886 Sunderland AFC paid their full expenses of £8 19s, *and* made a three quid profit. There was an additional bonus. The Scots won only by 2–1.

Not that finances were especially shaky by 1886. The shipbuilding Thompson family had become club members, and a certain ambitious organisation was beginning to distinguish Sunderland AFC from its neighbours in Durham and Northumberland.

The ambition made itself evident in many ways. There was not yet any league competition of any kind – the very idea of clubs forming into groups and playing each other for points at home and away had not been realised at local or national level in 1886. The only competitive matches available to Sunderland, therefore, were in the Durham and FA Cups. They tended to do well in the former, but last only one match in the latter. As a result, the only way of regularly facing top class opposition was to play friendlies.

This meant two things. Firstly, even if the clubs who travelled to Sunderland for friendlies were Scottish amateurs, there needed to be a substantial support on Wearside to pay their expenses. Luckily, Scottish amateurs were among the best practitioners of the game at the time, and they were at least as close to Sunderland as any professional outfit from Lancashire, so there was no shortage of good opposition.

And in their part, Sunderland were expected to return the compliment and travel to away games. On 27 February 1886 they did just that, leaving Wearside at 5.30 that winter morning to journey to play the oldest club in Edinburgh, the middle-ranking Heart of Midlothian. Hearts won 2–1, and Sunderland left with £3 in the treasurer's pocket.

In between playing St John's of Middlesbrough on 13 March 1886 (Sunderland won 6–0) and Darlington on 3 April (ditto, by 3–1), Sunderland Football Club moved ground once more, to the Newcastle Road stadium which would be their home for the following 12 years – and which would host the most consistent run of success in the club's history.

We can picture early home games at the Newcastle Road. Take the FA Cup first round tie against Morpeth Harriers in the autumn of 1886. In the close season the ground had been let out for grazing, but before this cup game club members went to work on the pitch with a lawn mower and a hosepipe. A new clubhouse was in the process of being built, but it did not provide changing facilities. Within a year or two the players would get into their new red and white kit at a nearby house on Ellerslie Road. In 1886, however, both teams had to make do with tents erected by the ground.

Before the Morpeth game, boys were hired to carry sandwich boards advertising the fixture around the town, and three policemen were employed at seven shillings the job lot to control the crowd of 4,000. Those spectators saw a goal-feast, as Sunderland won 7–2 to reach the second round of the zoned matches in the FA Cup for the first time. There they faced Newcastle West End, in a match which produced record gate receipts of twenty pounds. Sadly this match went into extra time – when, with Sunderland leading 2–1, darkness fell and it was abandoned. West End – who would shortly amalgamate with Newcastle East End to form Newcastle United – won the replay 1–0.

Sunderland continued to progress in the Durham Cup. They reached their third consecutive final in March 1887, once more facing Darlington, and won the trophy back by 1–0. But in between the local cup fixtures with Birtley, Gateshead and Whitburn, Sunderland were playing a very high class of friendly indeed. Over the Christmas and New Year season of 1886–87 the Wearsiders entertained Glasgow Rangers (beaten semi-finalists in that year's *English* cup!), Dumbarton Athletic and Linthouse – and had defeated the first and last of those Scots.

In the spring of 1887 they looked southwards, beyond the Durham border into England for the first time. After warming up with a defeat by Edinburgh St Bernard's, Sunderland faced Sheffield Town, Nottingham Rangers and Accrington. Only the last of those three was, in 1887, a club of any distinction, and Sunderland lost to all three of them – but it was a beginning, the club's name would henceforward be recognised in other parts of England.

The visit of Accrington in particular offered a signpost to the future. They appeared on 30 April 1887, the first professional club to arrive in Sunderland. Perhaps a little daunted by their visitors' reputation, Sunderland themselves paid a handful of Middlesbrough players three shillings apiece to strengthen their side. Accrington won by 3–1, but the significance of the occasion lay in the Newcastle Road crowd, and in the size of the gate receipts – fully £41, which was a Sunderland record.

Sunderland entered the 1887–88 season more determined than ever to make a mark on the English FA Cup. As if to stress their determination, Robert Thompson became president, his fellow shipbuilder James Marr took on the chairmanship, and the coalowner Samuel Tyzack was appointed treasurer. The club were now running a first and a second team (reserve home matches involved only one hired policeman, at a shilling a game). They prepared by paying the reigning FA Cup-holders Blackburn Rovers thirty pounds to travel to the north-east, and the top Scottish side Renton forty pounds to do the same. A massive ground expansion was planned. All seemed ready. And then, not for the first or the last time, they ran straight into trouble with the authorities.

Morpeth Harriers arrived once more for the first round, which Sunderland won 4–2 (Monaghan, 3). But Morpeth objected that the Wearsiders' full-back Ford had not been signed in time. The FA ordered a replay at Morpeth – which Sunderland won by 3–2 (Monaghan, 2).

Newcastle West End were dismissed without controversy in the second round. For the first time in their history Sunderland found themselves in the third round of the English national cup. They travelled to Middlesbrough, and came away with a 2–2 draw. No fewer than 8,000 people turned out to watch the replay, which Sunderland won by 4–2. There was immense excitement, as this third round signalled the end of the zoned matches, and the winner had a bye in the fourth round of the national competition – going straight into the last sixteen to meet Old Foresters at home.

But Sunderland went no further. The FA Cup had a long tradition of amateurism. During its early years only amateurs had been permitted to compete in it. In 1885 professionalism had been allowed, but with restrictions. Any professionals had either to have been born in the town they represented, or to have lived within six miles of their club's headquarters for the previous two years.

Middlesbrough were in 1887 an entirely amateur side (and they would remain so, on principle, until the end of the century). Sunderland quite clearly were not. Following the 4–2 Sunderland win at Newcastle Road, Middlesbrough protested that three of Sunderland's Scots – Monaghan, Hastings and Richardson – were not only professionals but also, far from 'living for two years within six miles' of Newcastle Road, travelled south on match days and were being lodged at the Royal Hotel at the club's expense.

A Football Association inquiry progressed from Darlington to London. Sunderland's board was furious, and allowed its heart to rule its head. Thompson, Marr and Tyzack must have known that they were in breach of the FA's rules, but at considerable expense they pursued the matter to a full meeting of the FA's council in London.

There, in January 1888, the FA's public school men examined the Sunderland books. They discovered 'a payment of thirty shillings in the cash book to Hastings, Monaghan and Richardson for train fares from Dumfries to Sunderland'. This was taken – doubtless correctly – as conclusive proof that the three Scots had not been loyal citizens of Sunderland for the previous 24 months. Sunderland were kicked out of the FA Cup and ordered to pay the expenses of the inquiry. Hastings, Monaghan and Richardson were each suspended from football in England for three months. And a bitter dislike of Middlesbrough FC was born.

This was a highly significant moment in the early development of Sunderland AFC. It established the club firmly in the ranks of those northern sides which saw their own future, and the future of the game of football, in professionalism. There can be no other explanation of Thompson, Marr and Tyzack fighting their corner so tenaciously and unapologetically, than that they considered that their club – while perhaps *technically* at fault – had committed no deep-seated moral wrong.

It was also a vivid illustration of the club's early reliance upon Scottish footballers. These were not men like the founder James Allan, Scots who happened to be living and working on Wearside. They were footballers who travelled south specifically to play for

Sunderland, and to be paid for doing so, or else to be found a good local job by the club as some form of compensation, or else a combination of the two. After White and Hunter from Kilmarnock, there arrived such talents as the stylish half-back Andrew Hastings. Signed from Queen of the South soon after the beginning of the Thompson/Marr/Tyzack reign in 1887, he was promptly selected for Durham County to play against Staffordshire, and – as we have seen from his involvement in the Middlesbrough FA Cup-tie controversy – was lodged in the Royal Hotel and paid travelling expenses between Scotland and the north-east. He will almost certainly have received a match fee.

(Andrew Hastings returned to Scotland before the club entered the Football League, but oddly – and uniquely – made a brief one-match comeback more than 20 years later, when he turned out at right-back at Roker Park on 24 April 1909 in a meaningless last game of the season against Preston North End! At least he was on the winning side that day: Sunderland beat Preston by 2–1, to finish third in the First Division.)

Hastings was quickly joined on the Edinburgh train and in the Sunderland squad by his compatriots Richardson and the prolific goalscorer Monaghan, and by the end of 1887 more than half of Sunderland's first team was Scottish. This obviously resulted in the displacement of several local players. Sunderland's growing support reacted ambiguously to this trend. On the one hand they enjoyed watching the likes of Monaghan banging in the goals. On the other they regretted the absence of such popular local men as Arnold Davison, the right-winger who had helped them to win the Durham Cup earlier in 1887, but who would die – still a young man – in Sunderland Workhouse in 1910. The lines of a local ballad ran:

> Who played right well in former days,
> For love of play and honour's praise
> Before the dawn of the Scottish craze?
> 'Twas Arnie!

And finally, the Middlesbrough FA Cup affair resulted in a split in the club which could have been fatal. It was a curious disagreement. James Allan, the original member, had retired from playing during the previous season following an injury. Allan clearly felt that the argument with the Football Association had been poorly handled by Sunderland AFC, and had reflected badly upon himself and his fellow Scots – some of whom he was personally responsible for attracting to Wearside.

On 13 March 1888 Allan called a meeting at the old Empress Hotel. It was attended by some of the older club members and several of the Scottish players. The meeting decided to form a breakaway football club called Sunderland Albion. Allan took with him six first-team players, including the disgruntled Hastings, Monaghan and Richardson. Almost instantly, Albion engaged Sunderland AFC in a battle for the footballing heart of the area. Playing out of Hendon, where James Allan had first fielded the Sunderland and District Teachers' Association Football Club just nine years before, the new club fielded no fewer than four sides, and enjoyed some good early results.

Back at Newcastle Road, Sunderland's board responded by finishing off the new clubhouse and extending the ground's spectator capacity to one of 15,000 – easily the most comfortable and capacious in the north-east (the club's accounts for that year showed a total loss of £370 on a turnover of £670, and the debit was entirely owing to £500 spent on 'renovation'). They then looked north once more and signed the half-back Willie Gibson from Cambuslang. Gibson was quickly joined by six more Scots and war was declared on Sunderland Albion.

Sunderland AFC's board realised that money was the root of success. If Albion were allowed to overtake them in attracting paying customers, then Albion would inherit Sunderland's footballing world. That was the reason for Sunderland's extraordinary action at the start of the 1888–89 season.

Sunderland arranged a grand total of 49 friendly matches for 1888–89. They played a Canadian national touring side (3–0 to

Canada before 14,000 fans at Newcastle Road) and Bolton Wanderers, Grimsby Town and Sheffield Wednesday. To Wearside they attracted Glasgow Rangers, Greenock Morton, Renton, and the famous apostles of the amateur game, Corinthians. They also entered, as usual, both the FA Cup and the Durham Cup. Following a bye in the first round of the FA Cup, Sunderland beat Elswick Rangers and Newcastle East End to reach the fourth round of the most prestigious trophy in the world.

Then the bombshell burst. Sunderland AFC were drawn to play Sunderland Albion in the FA Cup fourth round. A few days later, the two clubs were also paired in the first round of the Durham Cup. Wearside was buzzing with enthusiasm and speculation.

And then Sunderland AFC withdrew from both competitions.

The reason for this bizarre behaviour, explained club chairman James Marr, was that cup ties 'had served their purpose' by making the game of soccer popular, and could now be abandoned. Besides, added Marr unconvincingly, 'the unhealthy excitement they cause renders the scientific exposition of football impossible'.

Although there was in fact – as we shall see – more than enough 'unhealthy excitement' in the air, Marr was fooling nobody: not the Sunderland public, not his fellow committee members, and certainly not James Allan's Sunderland Albion. This was, after all, the same committee which had fought furiously against expulsion from the FA Cup less than a year earlier, and which had re-entered both knock-out competitions in the close season. Sunderland AFC withdrew from those two sensational cup-ties because they could not afford to play Sunderland Albion. They could not afford to let Albion gain the huge financial boost which would certainly accrue from two such matches. And they could not allow the possibility of Albion winning one or even both of the games, thereby diverting a percentage of Sunderland's soccer support away from Newcastle Road.

The ploy worked. Indeed, it worked better than even Marr could have expected. After a string of ambitious friendly successes, Sunderland AFC invited Albion to meet them at Newcastle Road on 1 December 1888. The new stands were packed beyond capacity – 18,000 people paid to see the local favourite Arnold Davison open the scoring in what finished as a 2–0 win for Sunderland. The point was surely proven, and the prestige-value was incalculable. A few weeks later a return game was played at Hendon, and Sunderland won again, this time by 3–2 after being 2–0 down at half-time. Albion disputed the winning goal, a clearance from their keeper which hit the Sunderland forward Breconridge and rebounded under the bar – but the referee, who was not helped by the fact that there were no goal-nets in 1888, ignored defenders' protests that the ball had passed *over* the bar, and allowed the goal to stand. Albion's players stalked off the pitch.

And the beauty of it all, the crowning joy, was that neither Sunderland AFC (who could afford the loss) nor Sunderland Albion (who could not) saw a penny of the enormous gate receipt. All £160 of it was given by pre-arrangement to local hospitals. The cash was not all that ended up in hospital – Sunderland supporters, infuriated by Albion's walk-off, ambushed the players' brake in North Bridge Street. Albion's goalkeeper distinguished himself by catching many of their hurled stones, but he could not prevent one from hitting James Allan, of all people, in the eye. Allan was rushed off for surgery.

Sunderland Albion lodged a complaint with the Football Association about the 'brutal conduct' of Sunderland AFC's supporters, but it was dismissed following an inquiry held locally at the Grand Hotel. Relations between the two outfits were extraordinarily bitter, eclipsing for a time even the bad feeling with Middlesbrough and Darlington. Shortly after the stone-throwing incident the referee, W.H. Stacey, who was imported from Sheffield to officiate at the second Albion match, and found himself isolated in a sea of hostility, criticised the whole poisonous atmosphere. He wrote to the Sunderland committee member W.T. Wallace, suggesting that: 'Surely the tension between your clubs is "too tight" when it prevents you meeting the referee either personally or by deputy for fear of offence to another club.'

Matters were not improved when Sunderland Albion predictably went on to win the Durham Cup, which Sunderland AFC had come to regard as their own, but from which they had withdrawn. There was better news for Newcastle Road from the FA Cup, however, when Albion were knocked out by Grimsby Town (whom Sunderland AFC had defeated in a friendly on Humberside earlier in the season).

It was argued many years ago by Arthur Appleton, the BBC's 'Voice of North-eastern Soccer' in the 1950s and a keen historian of the local game, that Sunderland Albion's role 'was that of a valuable irritant'. Albion's very existence, suggested Appleton, 'spurred the older club to an overshadowing success'. Sunderland AFC certainly won the war between the two clubs. They did not meet again on the field of play until the Easter Monday of 1892, by which time Albion had built a cinder cycle track at Hendon and had become – clearly in a desperate attempt to diversify – Sunderland Albion Football and Athletic Co. Ltd. Sunderland AFC won 6–1. A few weeks later they played each other again for the fourth and last time. Anticipating only another slaughter, just 2,000 fans turned up. Sunderland won 8–0. Four months later Sunderland Albion went into voluntary liquidation.

Sunderland AFC emerged victorious from that gruelling war against their upstart rivals for one major reason. They were canny enough in the opening skirmishes, to be sure, dropping out of cup-ties and giving gate receipts to charity. But the chief reason for the superiority and greater attractiveness of Sunderland over Albion in the early 1890s, was that Sunderland were by then successfully competing in a football tournament of national prestige and dependable high quality – but Albion were not.

At the start of the 1888–89 season, while Albion and Sunderland were playing their friendlies and dropping out of cups, eyes elsewhere in England were fixed upon a new competition. The Football Association, which had been established in London in 1863 by the public school and amateur clubs of the south of England, was regarded 25 years later as being out of touch with developments among the professional sides of the midlands and north of the country. Early in 1888, William MacGregor of Aston Villa FC had written to five of the leading northern sides, suggesting that 'a stricter control could be kept on the game, and more attractive fixtures arranged, if ten or twelve of the more powerful clubs formed themselves into a League.'

On 27 April 1888 the first formal meeting of 'The Football League' was held in Manchester. Twelve clubs entered, paying an annual subscription of two guineas each. They were: Accrington, Aston Villa, Blackburn Rovers, Bolton Wanderers, Burnley, Derby County, Everton, Notts County, Preston North End, Stoke, West Bromwich Albion and Wolverhampton Wanderers. (Three others – Sheffield Wednesday, Nottingham Forest and Halliwell – also applied but were for the moment rejected.)

No London or southern club would even attempt to enter the Football League until five years later, in 1893, by which time the competition had 28 sides in two divisions – and it is significant that the first one to do so, Woolwich Arsenal, was an artisans' works team which had been started in 1886 by young men from the midlands, the north, and Scotland who were employed at the Royal Arsenal in Woolwich. Indeed, one of Sunderland's most remarkable footballers of a few years later was to rise from this cultural environment of northern workers set down in the metropolis.

Nor was there, in 1888, an application from the north-east of England. But Sunderland's immense itinerary of friendlies put them into increasing contact with clubs which were engaged in the first season of the Football League. They played Bolton Wanderers away and crashed to a 10–1 defeat, then attracted the Lancashire men back to Sunderland and went down by only 4–3. But they beat Everton 4–2, Middlesbrough 4–0, Glasgow Rangers 3–0, and Derby County 3–1.

Their most heartening results came in a four-match spell in the spring of 1889. The first Football League championship had already been decided, and the FA Cup final had been played, when the beaten cup-finalists and third-placed league team

Wolverhampton Wanderers arrived at Newcastle Road on 23 April, only to draw 1–1. Wolves were quickly followed to Sunderland by the double winners Preston North End, who had gone through the whole cup and league season without losing a single game. Preston had won the inaugural league with 40 points out of a possible 44 (there were, of course, just two points for a win back then) and finished fully 11 points clear of second-placed Aston Villa. Ten thousand people paid £205 to watch Sunderland dismantle Preston by 4–1. On 11 May Wolves returned for another 1–1 draw, and soon after that yet another founding league side, Accrington, drove up to be beaten by 4–0.

Those four games against top Football League clubs which resulted in two wins and two draws, ten goals scored and only three goals conceded, convinced the Sunderland committee, players and fans of their next course of action. In the close season of 1889 the club applied for membership of the second season of the Football League. At that time the bottom four clubs in the league were obliged to put themselves up for re-election, along with any ambitious newcomers. So Sunderland went into the ballot with Stoke FC, Notts County, Derby County and Burnley. The League membership, doubtless swayed as much by loyalty to its founding members as by a reluctance to travel to the far north-east, rejected Sunderland's claim. Indeed, Sunderland attracted only two of the 12 clubs' votes. Stoke, Notts County, Burnley and Derby County were re-elected.

So Sunderland were condemned to see in the next decade with another season of friendlies, and with only the competition of the Durham and FA Cups, which they re-entered. But the board were now determined to make such an impression upon the world of English professional football that any future claim of Sunderland AFC could not be ignored. Before the 1889–90 season Samuel Tyzack elevated W.T. Wallace to an executive position, and between them they made the initial crucial appointment of the first great days of Sunderland AFC.

In that summer of 1889 they found Tom Watson managing the

most successful of the two major Tyneside clubs, Newcastle East End. Watson – an inveterate football organiser – had previously done the same job with Newcastle West End, with Willington Quay, and with Rosehill. The attraction of Sunderland to this Geordie was obvious. In 1889 none of the Newcastle clubs were showing anything like the same degree of ambition. East End and the failing West End would not amalgamate into Newcastle United until 1892, and the town's one suitable ground, St James's Park, was an undeveloped bit of parkland compared to Sunderland's Newcastle Road stadium.

Sunderland's committee, on the other hand, made it perfectly clear to Watson that their short-term ambition was a place in the Football League, and their (slightly) longer term plan was to become the top team in England. In order to achieve these objectives they were prepared to spend whatever money was necessary. And, in the prevailing climate of the day, Tyzack, Wallace, Marr and Watson once again looked north. Scottish footballers were available, thanks to the illegality of professionalism in Scotland; they were ambitious, since there was no Scottish League as yet; and they were indisputably better than their English counterparts (between 1872 and 1889 Scotland had played England 18 times. Scotland had won eleven, four were draws, and England had won only three).

The role of the four or five men who ran Sunderland Football Club in the 1880s and 1890s was not as clear-cut as it would be 100 years later. Tom Watson, for example, was not a manager as the job description is understood today. He would neither sign nor necessarily select footballers. Tyzack and Wallace made most of the excursions to Scotland to assemble the Team Of All The Talents. A dangerous expedition it could be, too, with Scottish supporters increasingly infuriated by English clubs poaching their heroes: there are tales of exploring English football executives being stoned at Scottish railway stations and ducked in Scottish village ponds.

The club committee would not only locate, negotiate with, and finally sign their chosen players. Having done that, they also expected to have a large say in who was picked for the first team. Tom Watson's basic job was that of match secretary – he administrated the team's affairs, from firming up friendly fixtures to making sure the kits were washed. Only as time went on, and the committee learned respect for his wisdom and ability, would Watson's views on team selection and player transfers become admired, and his voice would consequently grow weightier than that of any other individual at Sunderland AFC.

The season 1889–90, the first great season of the Team Of All The Talents, was very much a year of preparation for the Football League. This was the season of 47 games, 34 wins, four draws and nine defeats. It was the season of the arrival of the flying Scots Auld and Spence, Gillespie, Scott, Campbell, Harvie and Hannah. Thirty-one of those games were played at Newcastle Road, where they were beaten only four times – twice by Glasgow Celtic.

They had beaten Blackburn Rovers, Bolton Wanderers and Middlesbrough before they travelled to Blackburn for the first round proper of the FA Cup. Hannah and Scott scored to make the score 2–2 after 90 minutes, but Blackburn won 4–2 in extra time. (Rovers went on to win the trophy.) There was some consolation in winning back the Durham Cup, beating Darlington yet again, by 2–0 on 22 March 1890. And the friendly visitors kept coming. League clubs Accrington (8–2), Aston Villa (7–2), Bolton again (1–0), Notts County (2–1) and Everton (3–2) were all defeated.

Sunderland AFC's second bid for league membership came on 2 May 1890, at a general meeting of the Football League in Manchester's Douglas Hotel. This time only three established league clubs were obliged to seek re-election: Notts County, Burnley and Stoke. As well as Sunderland, four other non-league clubs applied. They were Newton Heath (who would become Manchester United), Darwen, Grimsby Town . . . and Sunderland Albion, who were already competing in the lesser Alliance League.

The importance of this meeting cannot be overstated. If Sunderland AFC failed to gain entry, their future would be difficult. If they failed and Albion were successful, they might have no future at all. Sunderland sent two men to argue their case: chairman James Marr, and a former player, the Revd J. Hindle.

Hindle's pulpit experience was assisted by the solid case he was given to present. He listed the club's full and successful record of the previous season. He pointed out that 13 of those 47 games had been against Football League opponents, and that six of them had been won, three drawn and only four lost. He stressed the 8–2 and 7–2 hammerings of Accrington and Villa.

But Hindle and the Sunderland committee knew that impressive results alone would not count. The Football League's midlands and Lancashire membership was nervous of the travelling costs involved in admitting a club from the north-east. So Hindle made the point that those clubs would have to travel to Sunderland only once during the season – whereas Sunderland would be obliged, and were willing, to make the same long journey on 11 occasions. Finally – and, some have suggested, crucially – he told the Football League membership that Sunderland would put a lump sum towards every other club's travelling expenses.

When the vote was taken, Notts County and Burnley were re-elected. The bottom-placed club of the first two seasons, Stoke FC, were kicked out of the league. In the place of Stoke the Football League elected its first new member: Sunderland Football Club.

* * *

And so the Team Of All The Talents entered the Football League in 1890–91, the league's third season of existence. As we have seen, despite all the high expectations they emerged from their first three games with two defeats, two deducted points, and precisely nothing on the table. At the end of September 1890 Sunderland AFC sat at the bottom of the league.

Things improved steadily. On 27 September goals from Spence, Harvie and Scott gave the lads their first league point with a 3–3 draw at Burnley. (John Spence was then dropped, having scored three goals in four league games. The man who had scored

Sunderland's first two league goals spent a year in the reserves before being transferred to Newcastle East End, and disappearing into football obscurity.)

The first league win to be officially recognised came after seven games and seven weeks, with Johnny Campbell netting four in a 5–2 away win over Bolton Wanderers on 25 October 1890. The first home win came just a week later. Sunderland took the field at Newcastle Road against Blackburn Rovers on the day after their appeal against the Teddy Doig mis-registration punishment had been heard in Manchester. Sunderland's claim was that a twenty-five pound fine and deduction of two points was a trifle harsh for 'what was only a technical breach of the rules'. The Football League committee voted by six to four to uphold the punishment and dismiss Sunderland's appeal.

The following afternoon of 1 November was not Teddy Doig's first home game. That had come in a friendly against Cambuslang four weeks earlier, when 5,000 fans had given the new Scot a cheerful welcome. But the Blackburn game was his first big test in front of 14,000 spectators. The crowd was boosted by the facts that Blackburn had just defeated the league champions Preston and were themselves riding high in the league; and the town of Sunderland was desperate to witness a competitive victory. It saw the dawn of one of the truly great Sunderland careers. Over the next 14 seasons Teddy Doig would play a total of 456 league and cup matches for his new club. In several of those seasons he would miss not a single match. This magnificent character, who always chose to hide his premature baldness beneath a cap which buckled under his chin (if he lost his cap, popular legend had it, Teddy Doig would go to save the headgear before the ball) played four times for Scotland while with Sunderland. But for the ban on 'Anglos' at the time, he would surely have gained more international recognition.

Most crucially, with Teddy Doig's arrival was born the reputation of Sunderland's invincibility at home. Following those first two defeats at Newcastle Road, for the next six seasons with Doig firmly between the sticks, the club lost only one league game in Sunderland. Doig's presence meant also that only the two full-backs, the local man 'Dowk' Oliver (by November 1890 the club's longest serving first-team player) and the international Tom Porteous, were English. Not that the crowd cared that Miller and Campbell had come from Annbank and Renton, as these two scored the goals in a 3–1 win.

For a club which had become accustomed to hosting more than 30 friendly matches a season at their Newcastle Road ground, the league diet of just 11 home games was always – despite the bigger crowds – going to be a little thin for Sunderland AFC. During their first few seasons in the Football League, they supplemented their official programme with a steady trickle of exhibition matches against Scottish or non-league opponents. After the above-mentioned Cambuslang, for example, the Alliance League champions Nottingham Forest arrived on 5 November. It was a Wednesday, but due to the opening of the new town hall the district enjoyed a half-day off, and 10,000 turned up at the match.

Three days later it was back to the league, when 6,000 turned up to watch persistent Sunderland pressure failing to break down a sturdy West Bromwich defence, and had to settle for a 1–1 draw. There followed three away defeats, by one goal to Everton and Notts County, which two games sandwiched a dire 4–1 thrashing at Accrington on a bitter November afternoon in front of just 3,000 people – and Accrington had started with just 10 men! Not even a 5–0 friendly defeat of Newcastle West End, with Kirtley getting a rare first-team outing, could disguise the fact that by the middle of December Sunderland's hopes of winning the league in their first season had evaporated. From 12 matches and a possible 24 points, they had just two wins, three draws, and a mere seven points.

The turning point in the season – and indeed, the turning point in Sunderland's whole early league career – came on 20 December 1890. Since signing Jimmy Murray from Vale of Leven in October to fill the left-half slot so tenuously held by Gibson and Spence (which, as Murray had been capped, gave Sunderland a Scottish all-international half-back line), Tom Watson and the committee had held faith with roughly the same line-up. On 20 December they began to get the pay-back.

The Everton side which arrived in the north-east that day had been league runners-up the previous year, and were on course to take the title in 1890–91. In winning this, their first league championship, they would lose seven games. One of them was to Sunderland on Saturday 20 December.

It was a close-run thing. Heavy frost during the week meant that the pitch was covered with straw until just before kick-off. The start itself was at 2 p.m., some 15 or 30 minutes earlier than was usual for a midwinter match, which in turn meant that only a disappointing 7,000 fans were inside when the game began, although more arrived from work and from the pub as the first half progressed. And a tight first half it was, with Everton's international inside-right Freddy Geary consistently threatening. But Doig, Porteous and Oliver held on, while Wilson, Auld and Murray steadily got a grip on the midfield. The half-time whistle closed down a goalless first 45 minutes and, with the minutes ticking away, one single second-half goal from left-winger Davie Hannah – his first of the league season – gave Sunderland a memorable 1–0 win.

It had been tough and dour, but that was the Football League. This was not exhibition stuff against Cambuslang, or Durham Cup finals against Darlington, or gentlemanly county select affairs against Nottinghamshire. This was the first football league in the world, and all of its contestants were learning – some more quickly than others – that it was a war of nerves and attrition. You battled to survive, and you fought your way out of those deadly bottom three re-election places. If you lost the fight there were few ways back. It was not only possible to go limping to the wall; it was commonplace.

That would not be Sunderland's fate. A 0–0 draw was scraped away from Aston Villa; Wolves were taken by 3–0 in the midlands; Villa turned up at Newcastle Road and Johnny Campbell's hat-trick in a 5–1 win showed William MacGregor that the Team Of All The Talents was still ticking. Then, right on cue, champions-elect Everton arrived back in the north-east for the first round of the FA Cup.

This match was widely billed as 'the greatest cup-tie ever played in the north'. Sunderland's recent improvement in form had led many commentators to suggest that whoever won it would go all the way to Kennington Oval to lift the FA Cup. A trifle premature, perhaps – but as it turned out, not far wrong.

There were no favourites. It was pointed out that the league clashes between Everton and Sunderland had each resulted in a 1–0 home win, and Everton's position on top of the table was deemed to be cancelled out by Sunderland's home advantage. And so despite the rival attraction across the town of Sunderland Albion hosting the 93rd Highlanders in another FA Cup first round clash, an extraordinary 21,000 people – 6,000 more than the supposed ground capacity – paid £420 to squeeze into Newcastle Road on 17 January 1891. The North-Eastern Railway Company ran special excursion trains from all over the district to cater for fans from across Durham and Northumberland. This was indeed a taste of things to come.

As was the result. This game was close to being a Scotland versus England international. On the Sunderland team-sheet Doig, Wilson, Auld, Murray and Campbell had all been capped for Scotland. For Everton, the centre-half Holt and three of the forwards – Geary, Chadwick and Milward – were all established England players (Geary had netted a hat-trick against Ireland the previous March, and Chadwick and Milward would both score for their country in the months to come). This formidable strike force would see Everton finish the 1890–91 season having scored 63 goals, almost half as many again as the league runners-up, Preston North End. Freddy Geary himself would wind up with 20 goals from 22 league games.

Over the whole season, though, Johnny Campbell bagged more than Geary. The Sunderland centre-forward got just 18 in the league – but he collected another four in the FA Cup. The first of those was against Everton on 17 January.

Both Sunderland and Everton had prepared thoroughly for this match in the oldest and most prestigious soccer tournament in the world – a tournament which neither of them had won. Everton had arrived at the Roker Hotel the previous day. They woke up to find Sunderland under six inches of snow, but it was quickly shovelled off the pitch and by Saturday afternoon the playing surface was clear – clear enough for Johnny Campbell, after a goalless first half, to net the game's only goal in the second period to put Sunderland AFC through, by 1–0, to the second round proper of the FA Cup.

The result left Everton free to concentrate on winning their first league title – a trophy which was beyond Sunderland. But as well as giving the Wearsiders genuine hopes of lifting the FA Cup, that game proved something else to Tom Watson and his men. It proved finally that they could compete with and defeat the best. It showed that the discipline imposed by regular league matches paid dividends. In the years since Sunderland AFC's foundation in 1879 and before the establishment of the Football League in 1888, amateur non-league teams had done well in the FA Cup. Public school squads like Old Carthusians and Old Etonians had won the trophy or appeared in the final between 1880 and 1883. The Scottish amateur side Queen's Park were twice FA Cup finalists in 1884 and 1885.

But after the advent of the Football League only one non-league team got to the FA Cup final. That was The Wednesday FC from Sheffield, and they were beaten 6–1 in the 1890 final by the league team Blackburn Rovers (and in 1891 The Wednesday joined the league). The professional Football League lifted the standards of its members beyond compare. And Sunderland were now part of that process. The improvement was palpable. After that cup win over Everton, Sunderland won three, drew two, and lost just one of their remaining league games. It was not enough to put them in the running for the title – not this year – but it lifted them out of the re-election places and into comfortable mid-table.

They also set off on an exhilarating FA Cup run. Non-league Darwen were dismissed by two second-half Davie Hannah strikes. The third round aroused particular interest, for while Sunderland had been dismissing Darwen, Sunderland Albion were drawing with Nottingham Forest, another non-league side. Then, as Albion and Forest were fighting out two replays, the draw for the third round was made – and it put Sunderland at home to the winners of the Albion/Forest marathon. It was Forest, however, who came through, beating Albion 5–0 on the Wednesday before the third round ties.

So Nottingham Forest appeared in Sunderland on 14 February 1891 for what was effectively a quarter-final of the FA Cup – the furthest that Sunderland had progressed. The 16,000 fans were not disappointed. Sunderland simply overwhelmed the Foresters. Playing against a stiff wind in the first half, the Wearside squad nonetheless laid siege to the Forest goal. Only some inspired goalkeeping kept the score-sheet blank – that, and the absence of the penalty kick rule, for within a couple of minutes Campbell was fouled right in front of goal, and then a Forest hand-ball kept the ball out (but the visitors cleared both free-kicks). Jimmy Miller broke the deadlock after John Smith ran half the length of the pitch before squaring to Miller, who converted easily. John Smith was another Scot who had arrived from Kilmarnock the previous year and had come from the reserves into the inside-right slot half-way through the season. In the second half of the match the floodgates burst, Campbell collecting two goals and Miller another one, to make the final score 4–0.

Following the second-round results, it was yet another indication of how far the Football League team Sunderland had moved ahead of their non-league rivals Albion. And it put Sunderland AFC, for the first time in their history, into the semi-finals of the FA Cup. Here they met the other Nottingham club, County. Notts County had been founder-members of the Football League and in 1891, after two seasons at the bottom of the table, they were riding high (they would finish in third place). Both teams travelled to the Bramall Lane ground in Sheffield for the semi-final. Sunderland stayed overnight at Ilkley. Ten thousand Nottingham fans outnumbered the north-easterners in a 25,000 crowd, but John Campbell, Davie Hannah and an own goal saw Sunderland achieve a 3–3 draw.

The replay was ten days later, at the same neutral venue. On the Saturday in between the two cup games, England played their first international match in Sunderland, at Newcastle Road; Tom Porteous was given his first and only cap in the 4–1 defeat of Wales. Four days later a midweek kick-off reduced the cup–tie attendance to 16,000. And on 11 March 1891, a bitterly cold day with constant showers waterlogging the Sheffield pitch, Sunderland went out of the FA Cup by 2–0.

Notts County lost the final to Blackburn Rovers, a team against whom Sunderland had enjoyed some success. The Wearsiders consoled themselves by thrashing Preston 3–0 and Derby County 5–1 in their last two league games of the season, both at Newcastle Road. It had been quite a year. But not even Messrs Watson and Tyzack could have anticipated what was to come.

THREE

Best of British

1891–1898

Football League clubs would have more competitive matches in 1891–92. The competition was extended from 12 to 14 teams. Nobody was kicked out at the end of Sunderland's first season. Stoke FC – who had been replaced by Sunderland a year earlier – were re-admitted, and the Wearsiders' FA Cup victims Darwen joined up.

If Sunderland found 26 league games strenuous, they did not show it. Perhaps the most extraordinary thing about the 1891–92 season was that the club actually lost three of its first four games, all away from home. By the end of September Sunderland AFC was once more propping up the Football League.

What happened after that was simply phenomenal. Out of their remaining 22 league fixtures, Sunderland lost another two . . . and won 20. Once again, it all began with a visit to Newcastle Road of Everton FC. Watson and Tyzack had acted quickly to cut out the perceived weak points. Two more Scottish internationals were brought into the Team Of All The Talents. Jimmy Hannah, who had signed for Sunderland Albion from Third Lanark in 1890, had been bought from Albion just a few months later, in January 1891. Hannah had to wait until 3 October and that home league match versus Everton for his full début – but after that he became a fixture, combining especially well with his namesake Davie.

More significantly for the local support, the full-back Donald Gow was bought from Glasgow Rangers. Gow would replace the last north-easterner in the team, 'Dowk' Oliver. Oliver, the only remnant of the days before the 'Scottish craze', was picked for league and FA Cup games just five times that season, and in the following summer he was sold to the Northern League's Middlesbrough Ironopolis – the 'Nops', as this early Teesside outfit was known in the north-east.

So the 11 men who faced Everton after another bad league start on 3 October 1891 consisted of 10 Scots (seven of them internationals), and one Englishman – Tom Porteous – who had been signed from a Scottish club. As a result, it is possible to picture the type of football that Sunderland played in the early 1890s and to explain the reasons for its success.

Scottish footballers of the 1870s to the 1890s played a different kind of game to their English counterparts. The Scottish style was widely referred to as the 'scientific' game. Essentially, early English soccer was visibly derivative of rugby football. It laid great emphasis on dribbling skills, on individuals running with the ball out of defence or bearing down on the opposition's penalty area (where it was virtually unknown for an Englishman to pass the ball: the man who had made the run was expected to reward himself with the shot). Defence was a matter of default. Some of the first English sides actually adopted eight-man forward lines. All 'tactics', in so far as they had any, were devoted towards that mad rush on goal.

In contrast, the Scots had from a very early stage adapted association football into a prototype of the twentieth century game. The Scottish 'scientific' game involved passing the ball frequently between team-mates, having close relations between inside-forwards and half-backs, and moving forward together as a unit. Scots were also prepared to head the ball, both in attack and in defence, which was a skill largely spurned by early English footballers – as is indicated by the fact that the first English rules of soccer did not allow for a crossbar: the ball was not often enough in the air for such a thing to matter.

Clearly, Scottish players also possessed the speed and control to set off on individual dribbles when the situation called for it. So their game was much more variegated, much more adaptable, usually more entertaining, and – as a generation of English internationals discovered – far more effective. If the English had given birth to association football, the Scots adopted the game, raised and educated it. Sunderland did not play a team full of Scots because Tom Watson and the club's committee disliked Englishmen. They did so – in the face of some muted local criticism – because those Scottish footballers were far more sophisticated players than anything available locally.

Everton, and the rest of the Football League, were about to find that out for themselves. The first ten minutes of that auspicious game against the reigning league champions from Merseyside showed all of Sunderland's brilliant potential in microcosm. Twelve thousand fans watched the new full-back pairing of Gow and Porteous absorb early Everton pressure, with Doig mopping up a couple of shots both behind and in front of his defenders. Teddy Doig did not, in 1891, have to stay on his line, or even inside his area. Until 1912 the goalkeeper was allowed to handle the ball anywhere on the pitch. This often led to keepers being stranded well upfield, although their mobility was limited by the fact that they could take only two steps with the ball in their hands.

Then Sunderland took over. Inside-right Jimmy Hannah celebrated his début by picking the ball up in defence and racing the length of the field to force a corner, which was cleared. Then Sunderland's international half-back line began to control the midfield in combination with inside-forwards Hannah and Scott. In the 11th minute Sunderland won a free kick. It was swung into the penalty box, Campbell pounced, and the ball was in the back of the Everton net.

The visitors pulled one back, but a Scott goal gave Sunderland both points by 2–1. There followed three more conclusive consecutive wins against West Brom at home and away, and against Accrington, which lifted Sunderland up into the top half of the table. Then a visit to Blackburn ended in a 3–1 defeat.

And that was the last worrying league set-back for two whole years. A week after the Blackburn reversal, on 14 November 1891, Derby County arrived on Wearside. Derby were riding high in the league for the first time in four seasons. But they never stood a chance. Within minutes Johnny Auld planted a free kick on Jimmy Hannah's feet in the box, and Hannah smacked it home. Campbell and Miller then went close before Scott grabbed the second. Before the 5,000 crowd had stopped cheering Hannah fed Campbell, who made it 3–0. Goodall got one back for Derby, but straight from the kick-off Sunderland turned on the style. What one observer described as 'some capital heading' was indulged in by the home team, who then brought the ball down for Hannah to shoot just wide. Then Jimmy Miller, playing out on the left wing, made it four. Then Miller went on to make it five, six, and (with his own fourth goal) 7–1.

They were off! Burnley arrived next, and had the nerve to score first after some threatening but fruitless Sunderland possession. Gibson and then Scott somehow failed to equalise, and Campbell – who was having a rare off day – missed a sitter after being set up from the left wing. The equaliser came with Sunderland's first ever penalty kick. The Football Association had accepted a proposal from the Irish FA and written this new rule into the book in the previous close season. From the autumn of 1891 onwards, anybody committing a foul or a handball in their own penalty area gave away, not a free-kick, but a shot directly at the goal from a spot 12 yards out. So when Burnley fouled some unrecorded Sunderland forward in the box on 21 November, Sunderland duly appealed to the referee. They had to do that – until 1894 referees were not allowed to stop the play unless footballers appealed to them for a decision, upon which (rather as in cricket) the referee made a judgement. Hughie Wilson placed the ball on that new spot, paced back like the free-kick specialising half-back that he was, ran forward and made it 1–1. Smith got the winner in the second half.

One of the wonderful things about the record 13 consecutive wins upon which Sunderland were now embarked – 13 wins which took them straight to the top of the Football League for the first time, in their second season of competition – was how easy most of them were. Notts County, for example, one of the league's most accomplished sides and cup-finalists of two years earlier, got off the Sunderland train on 5 December having just beaten Accrington by a league record of 9–0. County put out virtually the same team at Newcastle Road, bolstered by one new signing on the left wing. Sunderland fielded their standard ten Scots and one Englishman.

Jimmy Hannah, by now firmly established on the right wing, got the opener after solid Sunderland pressure which had resulted in near-misses by half the forward line and by Wilson from right-half. Hannah then made it 2–0. Referee Ormerod (an Accrington man, but presumably beyond reproach) gave a dubious penalty against County, which this time Campbell converted, and Sunderland went in for the break 3–0 up – despite the fact that 'their passing [was not] of its usual perfect nature'. Wilson made up for not being given the penalty kick by scoring from open play in the second half, and the team which had seven days earlier notched up a league record score-line of 9–0, left Sunderland on the wrong end of a 4–0 thrashing.

A week later it was Darwen's turn to get it in the neck. Sunderland had gone from the bottom of the table to the top in three months and 13 league games. But after the visit of Darwen on 12 December it would be almost three more months before they played another league game at home – the rest of their December fixtures were away, and January and February were devoted to the FA Cup.

At this half-way point in their first league season, newcomers Darwen were doing fine. They had 10 points from their 13 games, and were fourth from the bottom – out of the re-election danger zone. But Sunderland were no longer playing football for sentiment. They were playing to win the league. So Darwen were destroyed. Firstly their keeper MacOwen fisted out a Scott shot and Miller followed up to score. Then Wilson headed in a Jimmy Hannah corner, Campbell hit the post, Miller shot just wide, and Davie Hannah – paired at inside-right with right-winger Jimmy Hannah – made it 3–0. Jimmy Hannah had a goal disallowed for offside, but after the break Miller and Davie Hannah added to their total, and Johnny Campbell collected two. The final score was 7–0. Darwen were dismantled not just on the day, but for the rest of the season. They won just one more point, finished bottom of the league, and failed to be re-elected (although the addition of a second division saved their league career for seven further years – the little Lancashire club was finally kicked out of the lower division in 1899).

Everton at their Anfield Road ground (they would move to Goodison Park the following summer) proved just as easy on 25 December, giving Sunderland a 4–0 Christmas present. Then 24 hours later, on Boxing Day, down in the midlands a rebound off Tom Porteous gave Wolves a 1–0 lead before Davie Hannah equalised, Wilson made it 2–1 from the spot (he and Campbell were interchanging penalty kicks), and Jimmy Hannah wrapped up the holiday season at 3–1. Sunderland entered the New Year of 1892 with 12 wins, no draws and four defeats, on top of the Football League.

The first round of the FA Cup was played on 16 January 1892. The visiting opponents were Notts County, the side who denied Sunderland a place in the final nine months earlier, but whom they had beaten comfortably in this year's league. Sunderland won the cup-tie 3–0. However County then complained to the FA about the state of the Newcastle Road pitch.

When the rumour of this objection reached Wearside there was something close to panic among supporters. It was assumed that County's protest involved Sunderland's Scottish professionals once again in a residency qualification controversy. Suspensions, fines, and another ejection from the competition were all gloomily anticipated. Therefore the news that the County appeal had merely been about a frost-hard playing surface, and the game was simply to be replayed seven days later (on a pitch which had meantime been covered with straw and sand), came as a huge relief. On a clear, bright, windless day 12,000 paying customers duly flocked into Newcastle Road once more, to see Campbell and Davie Hannah go close, and Scott hit the bar in the opening minutes. Smith then also struck the woodwork, and this time Jimmy Hannah slammed the rebound home. Johnny Campbell made it 2–0 shortly after a Scott goal was disallowed for offside. Smith made it 3–0, and before half-time Campbell completed the scoring with the goal of the game: collecting a pass from Jimmy Hannah, he shuffled effortlessly past two Notts defenders before drawing goalkeeper Toone (who was twice capped for England later that year) and slipping the ball beyond him.

Four–nil, past the best goalkeeper in England! Sunderland moved confidently on to the second round, away at Accrington on 30 January – and astonishingly, this tie had also to be replayed because of the weather. It had rained so hard in Lancashire that the ground was a quagmire. The referee deemed it unfit for an FA Cup match, but as 5,000 people had turned up, a friendly was played. 'The Wearsiders,' commented the local press, 'knowing that there was no importance attached to the issue, showed a disinclination to unnecessarily fatigue themselves.' Accrington won the friendly 1–0. A week later on the same ground, Sunderland won the FA Cup second round game 3–1.

Stoke then took a 2–2 draw away from Newcastle Road, but were murdered 4–0 in the Potteries replay. It had taken Sunderland six matches to get through three rounds. By the time they met Aston Villa in their second consecutive FA Cup semi-final on 27 February 1892, the Sunderland first eleven had played a match on each of the previous six Saturdays. This was strenuous, and may have been responsible in part for another defeat at Bramall Lane, where Villa won 4–1 in front of an extraordinary 30,000 spectators.

There was nothing left but the league, and Sunderland made sure of that in style. Over the next two months, between 1 March and 30 April precisely, they played ten league games. The Wearsiders won nine of them and lost one, scoring 35 goals in the process. They clinched the league with three games to go, beating Blackburn 6–1 on Wearside. Campbell scored four that day, and three the following Saturday in a 7–1 thrashing of Darwen. The centre-forward from the 'Renton charge' finished the season as the Football League's top scorer with 32 of Sunderland's astonishing 93 goals.

This was a phenomenal goal-scoring outfit. To put it in perspective, four years earlier Preston North End had won the first league title undefeated, 11 points clear of the runners-up, by scoring an average of 3.36 goals per game. They netted 3.22 goals per game a year later, and new champions Everton managed 2.86 as the league defences bedded down in 1890–91.

But Sunderland won the title in 1891–92 with 3.69 goals per game. Johnny Campbell himself scored 1.23 goals per game, and registered another six in the five official cup ties. Jimmy Miller spent almost half of the season on the left wing, and netted 16 league goals. Jimmy Hannah started the season late, but logged 17 strikes in 19 matches, all from the right wing. The inside-forwards Davie Hannah, Smith and Scott got fewer, but that was more a reflection of the side's 'Scottish' scientific tactics than their own abilities – as inside-forwards for Sunderland AFC, they were expected to spend as much time helping out in midfield and even in defence, as in the opponents' penalty area. Wilson and Auld were responsible for 11 goals from midfield – although some of Wilson's were penalties.

And it must be borne in mind that Sunderland were still playing almost as many 'friendlies' – or invitation, exhibition matches, as they were known in the 1890s – as league and cup fixtures. In the championship and semi-final season of 1891–92 the players took part in a grand total of 58 games, only 33 of which were in the Football League and FA Cup. They won no fewer than 46 of those 58 games (although one particularly unpleasant defeat was by 4–1 at the hands of Newcastle East End in a December snowstorm at

Heaton – perhaps the Geordies could learn to play football after all). In all the matches played that season, Sunderland scored 217 goals and conceded just 69.

It was impossible to believe, but even better was to come. In the close season two old favourites returned. Jimmy Gillespie, who had left the Team Of All The Talents out of frustration at being unable to hold down a regular place, and had signed for Sunderland Albion, was welcomed back after the decline of Albion and – more pertinently – the sale of John Smith to Liverpool. Also John Harvie, who had temporarily returned to Clyde, was re-signed two weeks into the season. And another Scottish international full-back, Rob Smellie, was bought from Queen's Park after Donald Gow became homesick and returned to Glasgow. (Gow would see the light, however, and come back a year later to offer four further seasons of useful service in the defence of the red-and-white.)

The league had been massively extended in the 1892 close season. A 12-team second division was formed, into which dropped bottom-placed Darwen. And three new clubs – Nottingham Forest, The Wednesday of Sheffield, and Newton Heath (who became Manchester United in 1902) – were admitted to Division One, to make it a 16-club, 30-match tournament.

Sunderland started as if there had been no break, no change, no extension. They just picked up the pieces and continued as they had left off, with a 6–0 win at Accrington. Notts County then visited Wearside for the first home game of the 1892–93 season, with Sunderland already on top of the league on goal-average. Six thousand fans turned out on a warm September afternoon to see County take a 2–1 lead in at half-time, but goals from Campbell and Wilson dredged a point.

That was the last error for almost two months. The following Saturday Jimmy Gillespie and John Harvie made their come-backs at Aston Villa's home ground at Perry Barr. Sunderland won 6–1 in the midlands, and well though Harvie performed for his single goal, the game went down in history as one of Johnny Campbell's greatest matches. Although the centre-forward scored only two of the six, his all-round forward play, bringing his colleagues into the game and devastating the Villa defence, was the major reason for this destruction of a side which Sunderland feared, above all others, might wrench their title away.

Then came Blackburn Rovers. After the 6–1 triumph at Villa, it was reported locally that the Rovers players, who arrived by train on Friday afternoon for a good night's sleep in a Sunderland hotel, would not be overly optimistic – 'the football enthusiasts of Wearside were loud in expressions of their opinion that the colours of Rovers would be lowered.' And so they were, after a shaky start which saw the visitors make the only serious attempts on goal. Then Jimmy Hannah, Harvie and Campbell thumped shots in fom the edge of the box in quick succession, only to watch them rebound off Blackburn defenders.

Then was scored one of the goals of the season, and possibly the Wearside goal of the decade, for it summed up all that those Sunderland Scots had given to the English game. Miller, Jimmy Hannah and wing-half Gibson worked the ball down the left flank 'by combinations such as is seldom witnessed on any football field'. Gibson dropped off, leaving Miller and Hannah confronted by one defender. Miller slipped the ball inside to Campbell, who passed it back to Hannah – by now drifting across the edge of the box – and Hannah played it into the path of the lurking, unmarked inside-right, John Harvie. From inside the corner of the area Harvie then scored 'with unerring aim one of the coolest goals ever scored on the ground', and the 8,000 fans were uproarious. Two more from Campbell and one from Miller wrapped it up at 4–0, but the fans left talking of the first and best of them, that result of rare 'combination'.

Stoke and their five internationals were then dismissed 3–1; Everton were destroyed 4–1 on Merseyside. Then poor Accrington returned to Newcastle Road to concede an early goal when the two Hannahs tore upfield to lay on a stinging shot – the first of his hat-trick that day – from Campbell, and the champions won 4–2.

Just to emphasise their right to that place on top of Division

One, Sunderland then entertained West Bromwich Albion. West Brom were no mean side. They were the reigning cup-holders, and were in the top half of the league. Sunderland beat them 8–1, with a second Campbell hat-trick in consecutive games, two from Jimmy Miller, and to stress the diversity of the team, one from left-winger Jack Scott, and one apiece from the half-backs Wilson and Gibson. After eight games played, Sunderland were top of the league with seven wins and a draw, having scored 38 goals and conceded eight.

A couple of unexpected defeats – at The Wednesday and Notts County – slowed them down, and lowly league newcomers Nottingham Forest were only overcome 1–0 in Sunderland thanks to an early Campbell goal and some fine Doig saves. Yet that only served to add spice to the big league game of the year: the visit on 17 December of Preston North End. Preston were still a legendary outfit, if only for having won the league and cup double in 1889 and the league again in 1890 – just two and three short years before. In the previous two seasons they had been runners-up to Everton and Sunderland. Beating Preston meant something more than just another two points for any championship contenders – it set a kind of seal upon their aspirations, like murdering Caesar.

There was another factor. In the December of 1892 Sunderland may have sat on top of the league, but a revitalised Preston North End skulked dangerously in second place. Curiously – and this is yet another indication of the influence of Scots upon English professional football in the early 1890s – the local press made much of the fact that Preston North End had fewer Caledonians in their side than had most other big Football League teams: 'only six of [the Preston line-up] hail from across the border'.

A big crowd was expected. While the Newcastle Road official capacity was of course just 15,000, it had long been demonstrated that the ground could hold 20,000 without actually bursting at the welded seams. On 17 December 1892 Tom Watson laid on extra pay-boxes and opened up new entrances. They were needed. The kick-off was scheduled for 2.30 p.m., and from 1 p.m. onwards huge crowds had merged along the main road from the centre of Sunderland to the stadium. These were augmented along the way by the residents of Monkwearmouth and Southwick, and by the occupants of the ten freight trains which had shunted into Sunderland that lunch-time, filled with the fans of the rural outskirts.

'To say that the excitement concerning the match was phenomenal,' judged the local press, 'would not be an exaggeration . . . for it was felt on all hands that the result, whatever it might be, would greatly affect the future progress of the two splendid clubs who now, after several months' play, were running a neck-and-neck race at the head of the competition.'

In other words, win this one and win the league.

Inside Newcastle Road sixpence got you into the stand behind the goals. These places quickly filled up in the hour and more before kick-off. Places on the terraces along the side of the pitch went for one shilling, one-and-six, two-and-six and – for good central grandstand seats – as much as five shillings, or the equivalent of £13 in the year 2000. No fewer than 25 policemen were on the field, accompanied by a small detachment of soldiers, ready to keep the peace if needed. They were not needed. The capacity crowd remained excited and boisterous, but law-abiding. In the grandstand, in the five shilling seats, sat the Earl of Durham and his brothers, Claude and Francis Lambton.

Along with everybody else the Lambton family fell silent as the referee tossed up for ends on this fine, dry and mild December day. Then the whistle blew and the roar commenced, and Auld was driving Sunderland forward, and a Campbell shot was saved; and North End rallied and hit back, and the game was swinging to and fro at such a tremendous pace that local newspaper men pinched themselves to see that only five minutes had passed when Preston won their second corner.

North End were having the better of it. Sunderland were kept in the game by four remarkable saves in succession by Teddy Doig, who was half-way through what would become a record 108 consecutive competitive appearances for Sunderland in three and a half seasons, and having his best home game since signing. Preston dominated the first 30 minutes. Then the balance swung Sunderland's way. Watson's Scots put the visitors' goal under tremendous pressure during the last third of the first half – at one point, a cannonade of shots was struck repeatedly from close range against North End's defenders until Jimmy Gillespie put it wide. And in the second period a strike apiece from the two Hannahs, Davie and Jimmy, paired together at inside- and outside-left, gave Sunderland the points by 2–0.

It was not all jam from there on in. On Boxing Day 1892 the team was outplayed and thoroughly beaten 2–0 by lowly Wolves on an ice-hard pitch in the midlands. But that would be their last league defeat for another ten matches, by which time the second successive title was sewn up. That brilliant, unstoppable run – involving the kind of confident, all-conquering momentum which Sunderland were trademarking – began with an instant opportunity to take revenge on Wolves in the home league game in a snowstorm on 2 January 1893. Wolves were pulverised in a first half that had actually seen them take the lead. But after a Harvie shot was well saved, Jimmy Hannah equalised. The left-winger then made it 2–1; the snow cleared up and instead a flurry of shots besieged the Wolverhampton goal before Miller – standing in at centre-forward for the absent Campbell – got the third. Davie Hannah made it 4–1 before half-time, and in the second half Jimmy Hannah completed his first Sunderland hat-trick in a 5–2 win.

A 4–3 defeat of Everton at Newcastle Road on the following day, 3 January (after Sunderland had been 3–0 up), and a superb 2–1 win at Preston on 7 January (Sunderland's third game and third win inside six games, thanks entirely to two Jimmy Gillespie goals from corners in the first ten minutes), established the Wearsiders as hot favourites to retain the championship.

Then came Aston Villa, third in the table, on 14 January. The previous year's FA Cup semi-final had been partly avenged by that

6–1 win at Perry Barr earlier in the current league programme. But as with the Preston match a month earlier, this game was not only a four-pointer, a valuable chance to rack up a win and set back a challenger simultaneously. It was also a prestige match, a game against one of the established aristocrats of the English game. Since that 6–1 thrashing in September Villa had recorded an impressive series of results. On the previous Saturday, while Sunderland were beating Preston, Aston Villa had hammered fourth-placed Sheffield Wednesday by 5–1.

If there was any doubt about who was in charge here, it was quickly dispelled. Only 7,000 people saw it, but Sunderland murdered the midlanders 6–0. Davie Hannah got the first, and the second was a memorable goal, entirely characteristic of this team. A passing movement, which began with full-backs Porteous and Smellie, ran the full length of the pitch without a Villa player touching the ball. Jimmy Hannah picked it up out on the wing; his shot hit the post, rebounded into play, and Jimmy Gillespie placed it into goal. Gillespie bagged his second before the break, and Campbell, Davie Hannah and Bob Smellie made it 6–0 by full-time. (It was the Scottish international full-back Smellie's only goal for Sunderland in this, his one season in English football.)

With the league apparently sewn up, popular wisdom judged that by late January 1893 Sunderland were ready to make a meaningful assault on the FA Cup. Confidence was boosted further when the draw for the first round proper sent the Royal Arsenal of Woolwich up for their first visit to the north-east.

Thanks to the hundreds of men from the north and Scotland who worked there, the Royal Arsenal was the first professional soccer club in the south of England. (One of those workers, indeed, was a certain Aberdonian blacksmith named Buchan, whose four boys would grow up as Arsenal fans and aspiring professionals themselves – much, as we shall see, to the benefit of Sunderland AFC.) At the end of this 1892–93 season, in fact, Royal Arsenal would be admitted to the second division of the Football League, thereby showing the way to the rest of the south. But in

January 1893 Royal Arsenal were still a non-league club. Sunderland were English champions – and it showed. Sunderland's superiority (and implicitly, the runaway higher quality of northern league football over the game in the south) was evident from the start. Up 5–0 at half-time, the Wearsiders slackened off in the second period and won by only 6–0 (Miller 3, Campbell 2).

On 4 February the lads left the north-east for what could have been an extremely tricky tie. They were drawn away to Sheffield United, who topped the new second division. United, and second division football, presented an unknown quantity to Sunderland. They also had an exceptionally good defensive record. The north-easterners need not have worried. Miller and Campbell made sure of a 3–1 win.

Then came Blackburn Rovers away in the third round, with 20,000 Lancashire spectators and a 3–1 defeat at the hands of the club which Sunderland had beaten 5–1 and 6–0 in their last two meetings. The FA Cup certainly was a different country.

The league was won, though, and won comfortably. At a time when just two points were awarded for a win, Sunderland finished the 1892–93 season with 48 points from 30 games – equalling Preston's 1888–89 record of an 11-point advantage over the second-placed team (who were, once more, Preston North End themselves), but in a bigger and far more difficult competition. And this time the achievement was perfectly balanced. Champions of England Sunderland had the best defensive record in the league, as well as scoring the most goals. They scored, in fact, exactly 100 league goals – the first team to do so, and the last team to do so until almost 30 years later, when West Bromwich Albion won the title with 104 goals – but West Brom played 12 more games.

Once again the goals were spread all over that multi-talented forward line. Half-backs Wilson and Gibson collected 11 between them. Davie Hannah collected seven goals in 19 league games; Jimmy Miller 11 in 21 (although Miller also netted five times in two cup matches); Jimmy Gillespie 12 in 23; and Jimmy Hannah 19 in 27.

But the king of the goalscorers once again, not only in Sunderland but in the whole of England, was Johnny Campbell with his 28 goals in 27 league games, and three cup goals in as many cup ties. Campbell was a goalscoring phenomenon: perhaps the first great striker of the English league. Preston North End had a forward named Jimmy Ross who, back in that club's first two championship seasons at the beginning of the league, had scored roughly a goal a game. But Ross then disappeared from view. Campbell, on the other hand, retained his touch season after season. It is no coincidence that when Johnny Campbell topped the goalscoring charts, his club won the title.

Campbell was a man of medium height and solid build (over 12 stones in weight) and a rounded, youthful face, who looked likely to run to fat if spared training. Any examination of his career indicates that he had the born striker's predatory sense of position, coupled with a killing burst of speed, a fierce shot and all of the physical attributes necessary – particularly in the 1890s – to bundle full-backs, goalkeeper and all off the ball when necessary.

Curiously, because of the number of badly recorded friendly matches played at that time by Sunderland, the true extent of Campbell's achievements may never be known. In 1891–92, for instance, when Sunderland won the league with 93 goals scored, the team actually played as many matches again in 'exhibitions' and scored a season's total of 217. One of Campbell's most famous opponents, the Burnley, Aston Villa and England star J.W. Crabtree, later reckoned that Johnny had personally scored more than half of those 217 goals in one season.

As it is, Johnny Campbell stands at fifth in the certified list of Sunderland's all-time great goalscorers – in number of goals scored. But if we do the sums in another, equally telling way, and calculate the striking average per game, the figures show a different story. Only one footballer in the history of Sunderland has, over a long period, a better strike rate. Between 1925 and 1930 the remarkable Dave Halliday hit 162 goals in 175 league and FA Cup games – an average of 0.92 goals per match. Johnny Campbell lies just behind

Halliday, with 150 goals in 215 appearances, or 0.69 goals a game. Then, and only then, with around 0.5 goals per game, come the other great names: Gurney, Buchan, Holley and Carter. By any standards Johnny Campbell, the leader of the 'Renton charge', was a magnificent goalscoring centre-forward.

Campbell's strike-rate slipped in 1893–94, and that may have been enough to cost Sunderland the league title. The Wearsiders were certainly there or thereabouts for most of the season, knocking on the door at the top of the table, threatening to complete their hat-trick of championships. But it was another terrible start – for the team and for Campbell – that lost the title at the outset. Sunderland won just one of their first six games. Johnny Campbell scored just once in that period, and that was the consolation goal in a 7–1 thrashing by Everton in Liverpool. But it was Villa, not Everton, who dumped their season's hopes. Aston Villa took three out of four points from Sunderland in the league, and knocked them out of the FA Cup in a second round replay. And Aston Villa it was who took the league title, six points clear of Sunderland in second place.

Changes were made in the 1894 close season. Robert Thompson stepped down from the board and was replaced as president by the local councillor James Henderson. The executive was also re-shaped to admit a number of local worthies who between them guaranteed the club £1,100 (almost £60,000 in 2000) in spending money. This was necessary. Players' wages alone in 1893–94 had amounted to £3,400, and travelling had cost almost another £1,000. It was noted with some anxiety by the board that attendances had fallen in the previous year. A moulders' strike on Wearside in the late summer had caused further worry about crowd numbers, 'seeing how entirely the Wearside borough is composed of the working classes', but by September and the first game of the season that strike had been settled and hopes were expressed that the district might enjoy a calm and rewarding football season.

On the playing front the major change was the replacement of the immensely influential, but ageing, captain John Robertson Auld with another Scottish international centre-half, Andrew McCreadie. The newcomer McCreadie, who was signed from Glasgow Rangers, was something of a change from the tall figure of Auld – he stood just 5'5" in his stocking feet. Auld himself was reinstated as an amateur; but he stuck around with the club, playing in the reserves, until 1896, when he became the first Sunderland player to be transferred to Football League newcomers Newcastle United. After a handful of matches at St James's Park, the experienced Scot was shifted upstairs to the United board.

McCreadie was joined in the summer of 1894 by two more northern imports: the international full-back Bob McNeill and the wing-half Harry Johnston, both from Clyde. They arrived hard on the heels of the inside-forward Tommy Hyslop, yet another Scottish cap, who had signed earlier in the year. Otherwise the line-up was familiar. The Team Of All The Talents was not dead yet.

And what a start was made in the season 1894–95! Derby County (then known not as the Rams, but as the Peakites), who had finished third in the previous year's league, just two points behind Sunderland, were the opposition at Newcastle Road on the first day of September. The entire Sunderland forward line – Jimmy Gillespie, Jimmy Miller, Johnny Campbell, Tommy Hyslop and Jimmy Hannah – scored in a resounding 8–0 win. Maximum points were then taken from Burnley, champions Villa, and West Brom.

By Christmas Sunderland were established back at the top of the league. But Villa and Preston North End were still threatening – and in one of those interesting quirks of which the fixture list is fond, those two challengers were due at Newcastle Road in quick succession, on 1 and 2 January 1895. Preston were beaten 2–1, and a thrilling, see-saw contest against Aston Villa 24 hours later resulted in a 4–4 draw in front of 12,000 people, the biggest home gate of the season so far. In those two matches, Jimmy Miller scored a crucial five goals.

In February and March 1895 came the late-winter diversion of the early rounds of the FA Cup. Sunderland had an extraordinarily comfortable first-round home tie against unknown hopefuls Fairfield, and Miller got five in the predictable 11–1 win.

After that there were no more easy draws. Title-chasers Preston North End, Bolton Wanderers and Aston Villa came out of the hat in quick succession. Preston and Bolton were duly dismissed – but in the semi-finals it was Villa once more who knocked Sunderland out of the FA Cup. This time Villa went on to win it, beating West Brom 2–0 in the final at Crystal Palace.

And Sunderland went on to win the league, their third title in four years. Their third title, in fact, in only five years' presence in the Football League. Beyond dispute, Tom Watson had built the Team Of All The Talents into the greatest football club in England – by implication, in the 1890s, the greatest club in the world. Nothing seemed beyond them. A steady trickle of new signings would gradually replace the older players in a staggered manner, to maintain the spirit and the shape of the team. Crowds would remain steady. Improvements could be made. The FA Cup would surely be won. The future was bright.

The decline, when it came, was sharp and painful for being so unexpected. It is possible that, in the middle of the 1890s, nobody had anticipated the cruel and fickle nature of league form. Perhaps the Sunderland committee had assumed that football would work like a late-Victorian business venture: the more you put in, the greater profit you took out; success would breed success; trophies and profit would accumulate irresistibly along the way.

Perhaps they did not realise that sport was not like that. League football was not an ever-expandable business market. It was a sealed unit, in which only one body could triumph. Success depended as much upon confidence and strange unquantifiables like form, and tactics, and even luck. If those slipped from the grasp, they could not easily be replaced. Money would help, but money could never guarantee achievement.

Sunderland certainly slipped. They finished fifth in 1896, and Tom Watson, the secretary-manager who had led the club to what would prove to be its most successful period in history, decided to call it a day. Watson had opened a tobacconist's shop opposite Monkwearmouth Station in 1894, clearly with an eye on retirement. A reshuffling of the board and a reissued share capital combined with the team's lack of form and a marked fall in attendances to persude Watson to leave sooner rather than later. The tobacconist's shop was put on hold, however, for Tom Watson accepted an offer from Liverpool FC, recently promoted to Division One.

His job was taken by the Sunderland 'A' team manager, Robert Campbell, and by a new trainer, Billy Williams. Campbell's first season, 1896–97, was almost catastrophic. Their first eight league games passed without a win. Gates at Newcastle Road slumped to 3,000 and 4,000. The fault was not Doig's, nor even that of his fellow defenders. They conceded fewer goals than anybody else in the bottom six. The fault lay up front, where a forward line which had scored 100 goals five seasons earlier could only muster 35. They lost nine games by just one goal. On 16 April 1897, the last day of the season, they drew 1–1 at Bury to finish second from bottom of Division One.

Luckily, in 1897 there was no automatic relegation. Sunderland had a second chance. They took part in a play-off with the bottom team in Division One, Burnley, and the top two in Division Two, Notts County and Newton Heath. The play-off structure meant that each Division One side played the two Division Two sides at home and away. The play-offs began the day after the Bury match, on 17 April, and the four matches were to be played in nine days.

Sunderland lost the first, at Notts County, by 1–0. Two days later 10,000 people turned up at Newcastle Road to see them scrape a 0–0 draw – and a valuable point – at home to County. The tension was such that a member of the crowd died from heart failure during the game. Then they travelled to Manchester to draw 1–1 with Newton Heath.

Everything rested on the last play-off match, at home to Newton Heath on 26 April 1897. Only a win would do. At that point, after three games, Sunderland were placed bottom of the play-off group. Another draw would see them relegated. Robert Campbell and Billy Williams held their nerve and stuck by their players. That effectively meant that it was up to the Team Of All The Talents to preserve the pride and the standing that they themselves had given to Sunderland AFC – in their last game as a unit for the club. For everybody, including the players, must have known that win, lose or draw, relegated or not, this was the end of the line for the 'Renton charge' and its supporting cast. They were ageing; their venom had been sucked dry; they were playing on memory and pride.

But what pride! They delivered. One last time and when it truly counted, in an undignified bottom-of-the-pile scrabble for survival, they delivered. Two goals from Jimmy Gillespie were scored without reply. Newton Heath stayed in the second division, to think again and eventually to become Manchester United. And Sunderland stayed in the first division.

Then the team, and the old ground, broke up together. Campbell and Harvie both followed Johnny Auld to Newcastle United (now an aspiring second division outfit) for forty pounds. Miller had already departed for Glasgow Rangers. The two Jimmies, Hannah and Gillespie, went to Third Lanark. By late summer only Doig and Wilson remained of the great squad which had delivered three titles to Wearside. And chairman Henderson, showing great faith in the future of the club and noting keenly the massive league crowds of 30,000 and more which were now commonplace elsewhere, went in search of a new stadium.

The players that Campbell brought in were solid and able replacements. Sandy McAllister, yet another Scottish international centre-half, came from Kilmarnock. The inside-forward Jimmy Leslie cost forty pounds from Bolton Wanderers. The left-winger Colin McLatchie arrived from Preston. The Middlesbrough-born full-back Phil Bach was tempted from Southern League Reading, and Bach would proceed to win an England cap while on Sunderland's books. For with the end of the Team Of All The

Talents, there also died the heyday of the 'Scottish craze'. They were still there in plenty, of course, and they always would be. But by 1897 professional football was legal in Scotland. That fact combined with the increasing sophistication of native-born English players – they had picked up the Scottish tricks – meant that never again would a side consisting virtually entirely of *émigré* Scots win the English league. Not even on Wearside.

The new boys did well. Their results were solid rather than spectacular. No more victories by six, seven and eight goals were recorded. Derby County, for instance, whom the Team Of All The Talents had regularly beaten by 7–1, 5–1, and 8–0, arrived in Sunderland for a league match on 9 October 1897, when their hosts were riding high in the league, and found themselves 2–0 down by half-time. At that point the wind, which should have assisted Derby, dropped, and one of their inside-forwards could only play while injured. But the new Sunderland had neither mood nor will to rub it in, and Derby were surprised to be let so far back into the contest that they pulled a goal back before the end and could have snatched a point.

However they did not, and neither did too many other sides. A good unbeaten run throughout January and February saw the Wearsiders climb dramatically from the bottom half of the division into second place, and saw their home crowds elevate back to a respectable 10,000 on average. That was welcomed by nobody as much as the captain, Hugh Wilson – the home league game against Blackburn late in the season also doubled as his benefit match, to mark eight seasons of service. Ten thousand fans paid into Wilson's savings account and offered him a huge cheer, while no doubt reminiscing in bittersweet mood about those three championship flags which the wing-half-turned-inside-forward had helped wave over Newcastle Road. (And Sunderland beat Blackburn 2–1.)

Second place in the first division was a reasonable indicator of hope. The board celebrated in the summer of 1898 by preparing to move from Newcastle Road to a new ground with a capacity of over 30,000, which included 2,000 seats. The stadium had taken a year to build on old farmland. The stands were wooden, and the steps had an unusually high rise of nine inches, making its steep terraces excellent for viewing football. The pitch was laid with such high quality turf imported from Ireland that the playing surface lasted for over 30 years.

The name of this new ground would, over another century, become and remain famous. It was linked to the sound made by the most celebrated home crowd in Britain. It became a by-word for passion in soccer. It was called Roker Park.

FOUR

Triumph and Trauma

1898–1918

It was estimated that the new ground at Roker Park could hold 30,000 people comfortably; 40,000 at a stretch. It was baptised on 12 August 1898 with a local 'Olympic Games'. The modern Olympics had been revived two years earlier in Athens, and this was a great period for mini-mimic-Olympics. Twenty thousand north-easterners turned up to watch field and track sports at the new Roker Park – an attendance record for athletics in the region.

The proper christening of the new ground came a month later, on 10 September, with Sunderland AFC's first home game of the new season. The build-up to this match was enormous. Thousands of people had turned up to watch pre-season practice games to check that Billy Williams was right when he said that his men were 'in the pink of condition and training most assiduously' (6,000 fans turned up at the ground to watch their preparations on the Wednesday before the big day). Sunderland had won their first league fixture, away to Preston, seven days earlier by 3–2. The English Football Association had declared its willingness to locate either an international match or a cup semi-final at Roker in the coming season. (It turned out to be an international, on 18 February 1899, when an England side featuring Sunderland full-back Phil Bach beat Ireland by the record score of 13–2.) The Marquis of Londonderry was due to do the honours on 10 September – 'what strides,' effused the press, 'must a game that was once prohibited by law have made, to receive the countenance of one of England's aristocracy!' The game itself could hardly have had more fitting contestants. Tom Watson's new club, Liverpool, was due up on Wearside to play his old side. Thirty thousand paid to get into Roker Park on 10 September 1898. They went home happy: a fraught contest was finally decided 1–0 in Sunderland's favour, thanks to a late goal from Jimmy Leslie.

After three league matches Sunderland were neatly poised in second place, a point behind Everton with a game in hand. Thereafter the season went into mild decline. Aston Villa won the title once more, with Tom Watson's Liverpool a close second. In their first season at Roker Park Sunderland finished seventh, and were dismissed from the second round of the FA Cup by non-league Tottenham Hotspur.

Following the official opening, the 1898–99 season was memorable for at least one other notable occasion. At the end of the previous season Newcastle United had in their fifth year of trying finally gained promotion to Division One. Sunderland and Newcastle had regularly played each other in tightly-contested friendly matches (usually at St James's Park, to help United – and Newcastle East End before them – with funds). But on 24 December 1898 the two north-eastern clubs met for the first time in a competitive league fixture.

The game was at Roker Park, and 30,000 people paid to get in. Not all of them were from Wearside – 'every north country devotee of the dribbling code was present,' it was reported, 'either in person or in spirit.' The hefty Tyneside contingent travelled with great expectations, despite their league position five points beneath Sunderland.

Sunderland took the lead through Jimmy Leslie, when a rebound off Hughie Wilson's knee fell into the little inside-forward's path. 'The crowd, or rather the Sunderland section of it, went delirious with joy,' reported the press, 'and the players shook hands with each other all round.' But almost immediately United were level, when a William Wardrope shot gave Teddy Doig no chance. And shortly before half-time Jock Peddie gave the Geordies a 2–1 lead. Sunderland, having relinquished their advantage, seemed to lose their pattern, and Wardrope shook off Wilson's attentions early in the second half to make it 3–1 for Newcastle. Leslie pulled one back before the end – but a pattern was set which would last for decades. Sunderland had less trouble in beating United in Newcastle (which they did in the return fixture of this 1898–99 season) than in taking maximum points off the Geordies at Roker Park. Nerves, pressure, the unbelievable atmosphere of a packed north-eastern crowd – all seemed too much for the players on the day.

In the close season of 1899 Hughie Wilson decided that it was time to wind down his distinguished professional career, so he moved to non-league Bedminster. He was not the only man to go. Manager Robert Campbell took the offer of a job at Bristol City. He was replaced by Alex Mackie. Billy Williams stayed on as trainer, under Mackie, and for a number of years after Mackie's departure.

Alex Mackie and Billy Williams set about building a team for the new century. And they succeeded. The triumphs of the Mackie/Williams squad were huge. They came to within an ace of bettering the accomplishments even of Tom Watson's team ten years earlier, the team under whose shadow they and all subsequent Sunderland sides laboured.

They built on Teddy Doig, the veteran goalkeeper. Andrew McCombie, later to become a Scottish international, came down from Highland League club Inverness Thistle to occupy the right-back slot with enormous authority. Jimmy Watson, a 5'11", 13-stone left-back, arrived from Clyde. The half-back line was based on Matthew Ferguson from Mossend (who would tragically die in the summer of 1902 at the age of 29, immediately after his team's greatest victory); centre-half Sandy McAllister, Dicky Jackson from Middlesbrough; and the future club captain James William 'Billy' Farquhar, another Highland import from Elgin City.

In the forward line was the dashing, handsome Billy Hogg from

Willington Athletic. 'When they cease to play Willie for his football,' it was said locally, 'they may do worse than play him for his appearance.' Hogg's football was good enough – he would win three England caps in 1902. Jimmy Miller was persuaded to return from Glasgow Rangers and wear his old team-mate Johnny Campbell's number nine shirt. Local boy Alf Common flitted in and out of the attack before he became the first thousand-pound footballer when Middlesbrough bought him for that sum in February 1905. Then there was Colin McLatchie on the left wing and Jimmy Gemmell, yet another purchase from Clyde FC, at inside-left.

That was essentially the side with which Mackie and Williams assaulted the English league as the twentieth century was born. In 1899–1900 they finished third behind Sheffield United and champions Aston Villa – a season that was remembered as much as anything else for the fact that Manchester City's keeper scored his side's only goal in a 3–1 Sunderland win at Roker Park, beating Doig with a wind-assisted goal-kick!

In 1900–01 they edged closer to the title. The defence of Doig, McCrombie and Watson was easily the best in the first division, conceding only 26 goals in 34 games. But there were too many draws – 13 in all – which dropped points, particularly at Roker Park, and exacted a heavy toll in the final reckoning. Sunderland finished in second place, an agonising two points shy of Tom Watson's new champions, Liverpool.

And then, in the season 1901–02, ten years after their first title, Sunderland won the championship of the Football League once again. It was, however, a campaign quite unlike the triumphs of the Team Of All The Talents. The title-winning side of 1891–92 had scored 93 goals in 26 games. The team that Billy Williams and Alex Mackie drove to the top in 1901–02 netted a mere 50 goals in 34 matches. Their defence had a superior record to that of ten years earlier, letting in just over a goal per game, as opposed to just under a goal and a half a game. This fact was duly recognised when the goalkeeper and full-back combination of Doig, McCombie and

Watson were all picked together to fill those positions for Scotland. But the days of immense victories, of those five-goal margins, were well and truly gone. The Football League had bedded down. There were, among its 36 member clubs in two divisions, no more easy opponents.

It was altogether a different game, and it was played by a different kind of team. Sunderland's joint top scorers in that championship season of 1901–02 were Jimmy Gemmell and Billy Hogg with just ten goals apiece. The half-back line – once such prolific goalscorers for Sunderland – netted a season's total of just five league goals between them, less than Hughie Wilson used regularly to collect by himself.

Nothing illustrated this dramatic change better than the centre-half position. Replacing Andy McCreadie, with his ten goals in two seasons, and Johnny Auld, who once netted four in a campaign, was Sandy McAllister. McAllister was undoubtedly a great defensive number five, a true stalwart of the club who deserved his league champion's medal. But Sandy McAllister had played 110 games over three and a half seasons before he broke his duck and scored his first goal for Sunderland! The centre-half's baffling failure to find the back of the net became such an issue at Roker Park that a group of supporters banded together and promised to give the Scottish international a piano in exchange for his first goal. When Sandy McAllister did manage to score, in his 111th first-team game, a goal which won the team a point at Preston on 5 January 1901, the supporters gave him not only a piano, but also an expensive gold watch!

But success was success, however achieved. The 1901–02 league title meant that Sunderland Football Club had been English champions four times in only 12 seasons of membership – a record which outstripped that of any other side in the country. Two men were present in each of those four seasons. And one man alone had been there from the very beginning, been disappointed in all of those cup semi-finals, and had kept goal throughout all the 12 years of those four title-winning seasons.

Teddy Doig could claim to be the greatest servant in the history of Sunderland AFC. His total of 456 league and cup appearances has been bettered only by that other brilliant goalkeeper, Jim Montgomery. But including friendly matches – which were such an important feature in Doig's day – the Scot turned out between the Sunderland sticks a total of 674 times, 51 games more than Montgomery. And when the 37-year-old Teddy Doig finally left for his old boss Tom Watson's Liverpool FC on 12 August 1904 after 14 years on Wearside, he took with him the silverware and memories of four league championships. Doig was not finished there, either. He instantly helped the Merseyside club to return to Division One, after their relegation the previous season. And in his 40th year, his 16th year as an English professional, he played in Liverpool's very first division title-winning side of 1905–06. This goalkeeper was so remarkable that even while playing for Sunderland in England he won six Scottish caps, the last of them as late as 1903 when he was 36 years old.

If Teddy Doig's was the ultimate Sunderland career, Jimmy Miller – the only man who shared the first four league titles with him – had surely just the ultimate career. Miller arrived from Scotland, as we have seen, shortly before Doig in 1890. He was an integral part of the forward line of the Team Of All The Talents. Jimmy Miller played a full role in all of the first three championship seasons, as a prolific goalscorer and an adaptable goalmaker – Miller was so adaptable that during his Sunderland career he played in every one of the five forward line positions, and also turned out once or twice in the half-back line.

Following the legalisation of professional football in his native country, Jimmy Miller returned to Scotland to play for Glasgow Rangers in the summer of 1896, with three English championships under his belt. In his first season with Rangers, playing at centre-forward, he collected a Scottish cup winners medal, scoring twice in the final. He got another cup the following year, while playing mainly on the right wing. He then won two consecutive Scottish league championships with Glasgow Rangers before returning to

Wearside in the summer of 1900 – just in time to win yet another English league title with Sunderland!

Due to his time spent as a professional in England with Sunderland, Jimmy Miller won only three caps for Scotland. While with Rangers he played twice against England and scored both in London and in Glasgow. Between those two international fixtures he put on the Scottish jersey for a 5–2 beating of Wales in 1898. That Wales match was Miller's only international in which he did not score. He did, however, help to lay on a hat-trick for his former Sunderland team-mate Jimmy Gillespie, who – having moved on himself to Third Lanark – was finally making his own Scottish début.

Those were the veterans; the only men to span the two great championship sides of Sunderland's early years. They both arrived on Wearside in 1890 and they both left for the last time in 1904. In between, Teddy Doig and Jimmy Miller had helped the club to the most successful period of its distinguished history.

The title-winning team of 1902 had another season together, with minor alterations. Doig and Miller were still there, and still playing regularly, in 1902–03. And Sunderland came to within an ace of winning the title once more. They led the table until the middle of March, when they lost at home to Sheffield Wednesday by 1–0. Some controversial refereeing in this game resulted in a small group of Edwardian hooligans throwing rocks at the brake carrying the Sheffield players and the referee along Roker Baths Road to the station after the match. A court case resulted and, more dangerously, Sunderland were ordered by the Football Association to play their Easter home game against newly-promoted Middlesbrough (the very first scheduled Wearside v. Teesside league derby) at the 'neutral' venue of St James's Park, Newcastle. This meant that Sunderland, the league leaders, found themselves looking suddenly at a title run-in of four final matches, all away from Roker Park – and the last two, against Middlesbrough and Newcastle, at St James's.

In the event they almost lost the title before they got to

Newcastle. Twenty-five thousand turned up at Roker on 10 April 1903 for what was now the last home league game, against Stoke, but Sunderland could only grab a goalless draw. Next day they travelled to Bolton and lost 2–0, and on 13 April they lost 5–2 at Nottingham Forest. Astonishingly the cause was not yet dead. If they could beat Middlesbrough in the re-arranged 'home' game in Newcastle . . . And they *did* beat Middlesbrough, Jimmy Miller grabbing almost his last goal for the club in a 2–1 win.

So the destination of the 1903 league title came down to Sunderland's last fixture of the season, away at Newcastle United. The omens were good. Sunderland had won each one of their previous four away league games at Newcastle. They lost this one, of course, by 1–0 in front of 27,500 fans. Sunderland finished third in the league with 41 points, the same total as second-placed Aston Villa, and just one point below champions The Wednesday FC from Sheffield. A win instead of a defeat, in any one of those last three away fixtures, a couple of wins instead of any two of those nine draws – 'With just a shade of extra forward power,' wrote the BBC's sports reporter in the north-east 40 years ago, Arthur Appleton . . .

'With just a shade extra forward power – another two or three goals – Sunderland would have had a run of three championship successes, 1900–01 to 1902–03.' Well, yes – but you may as well argue that another two or three goals against the club in the same period would have put them quite out of the running! In a tighter league contest, the side of the first years of the twentieth century was not able to dominate in the way that its predecessor had done. Such opposition as Everton, Villa, Liverpool, The Wednesday, and even Newcastle United, was not only formidable: it was also sustained by massive home support. Crowds unprecedented in size were paying their way into professional football matches – 30,000 in Liverpool and Sheffield, 47,000 at Aston Villa. And they were hungry for more. Hungry not only for success but for new and fresh opposition.

It was not an easy environment in which to thrive. Some found it a difficult place in which to survive. Sunderland were not among the latter, but for a further ten years after 1903 they would be unable to recreate their league success.

The second great title-winning side was quickly broken up. As we have seen, Miller and Doig finally left in 1904. Matthew Ferguson died. Most damagingly, the great right-back Andy McCombie – with Doig such a pillar of strength in the defence – left prematurely and in demoralising circumstances which affected the club for years.

The McCombie story was a disaster in every respect. In the summer of 1903 the Highland international was given one hundred pounds by the new chairman of the club, Sinclair Todd, to help start a new business. Shortly afterwards McCombie was allowed a benefit match. When the player had banked the gate receipts, Todd asked for his hundred pounds back. McCombie said the money had been a gift, that it was quite unrelated to his benefit, and refused to return it. The matter festered until early in 1904. Then, on 23 January, McCombie turned out for Sunderland in a home league game against Bury. Sunderland won 6–0, but it hardly mattered: the side were marooned in mid-table, unlikely to regain the title. Only the FA Cup remained, and that presented a challenging first round tie at Manchester City a fortnight later.

Andy McCombie would not be there. The full-back had played his 164th and last game for Sunderland. When the squad travelled to Seaton Carew to train for the FA Cup tie, McCombie was noticeable by his absence. The immediate result was that the vultures descended: virtually every club in the first division promptly applied for the 25-year-old Scottish international full back's signature. But McCombie was unwilling to give up the business started with that fateful hundred pounds, and was consequently unwilling to leave the north-east.

So he signed for Newcastle United. Newcastle had earlier hijacked the signature of a friend from Inverness who had been on his way to meet up with McCombie at Sunderland in 1902, and on 4 February 1904 Andy McCombie joined Peter McWilliam at St

James's Park. He cost the Geordies a record transfer fee of £700, but it was a bargain. McCombie was no older player like Johnny Auld or Johnny Campbell before him, looking to see out his twilight years on Tyneside. He was a great full-back at the peak of his powers. Within a year of signing Andy McCombie, Newcastle United had won the league and reached the final of the FA Cup. McCombie played for Newcastle until 1910, helping them to a total of four cup finals and three league titles.

In the same period Sunderland achieved nothing. For the loss of Andy McCombie had even further repercussions. Following his transfer (and Sunderland's dismissal from that year's FA Cup by Manchester City), Sinclair Todd and his fellow directors took McCombie to court to try to reclaim their hundred pounds. The result was yet another self-inflicted wound by the officials of Sunderland AFC. For the court found in their favour: it ruled that the money had indeed been a loan, and therefore should be repaid by McCombie.

But this very public squabble inevitably attracted the attention of the Football Association yet again. What, they wondered, was Sunderland AFC doing handing over large sums of money to its players, as loans or as gifts? The FA held another inquiry into the club's affairs. Its results were shattering. In October 1904 the Football Association announced that it had 'sympathy' with Andrew McCombie for his part in the gift/loan affair, and no action would be taken against the footballer. The football club's position was, however, a different matter. The FA announced that Sunderland's account books did not show a true record – in other words, that they were cooked. They said that following their inquiry they were satisfied that Sunderland AFC were once again guilty of making illegal payments to players, chiefly bonuses for winning or drawing, and upon re-signing contracts. Sunderland Football Club were fined £250 (about £11,500 in 2000). But that was the least of it. Six directors, including chairman Sinclair Todd, were suspended for two and a half years and manager Alex Mackie was suspended for three months.

The result was a complete upheaval in the running of the club and in the management of the team. In the long term this would incidentally prove beneficial, but in the short term it was traumatic. Only one young director, a colliery agent and coal exporter named Frederick William Taylor, was left to pick up the pieces. Taylor did more than that. He served as chairman from 1904 until 1913, and he remained on the board of the club for a further 30 years, until after the Second World War. In the words of Bob Graham, an earlier biographer of Sunderland AFC, 'through his efforts the club was saved from extinction'.

It is in fact unlikely that the McCombie affair came close to killing the club in 1903 and 1904. It was too affluent, too successful and too established an institution to fall off the face of the earth. But Taylor pulled it together in a difficult period. He gave it complete security, for instance, by supervising the purchase of Roker Park in 1905. And when it became clear that a combination of the McCombie affair and mediocre results made it impossible for Alex Mackie to remain as manager, in the summer of 1905 Frederick Taylor replaced Mackie – who went to Middlesbrough – with Robert H. Kyle, the secretary of Belfast Distillery Football Club.

And so began the reign of Bob Kyle, which would become easily the longest managerial regime in Sunderland's history. It did not begin well, although there were bright spots. There was the goalscoring form of the left-sided forward Arthur Bridgett, who had arrived from Stoke in 1903. Bridgett – a devout religious missionary who toured the country discoursing on such themes as 'The Game of Life' – was a quick and ruthless striker with a shot so powerful that (against his old club Stoke) he once burst the net. He also became an England regular who netted three times for his country.

There was the ball artist George Holley, who was to become another England international, a local apprentice fitter when he signed from Seaham White Star on his 19th birthday in November 1904. As well as dazzling skills and an unerring eye for goal, 'Geordie' Holley was also capable of looking after himself.

Following one goalmouth tussle involving Holley, the opposition goalkeeper – Sheffield Wednesday's Jack Lyall – was left swinging upside down from a foot caught in the roof of the goal-net. Holley scored eight times for England.

And there was, in bursts, Alf Common. Yet another England cap, Common has become more famous for his transfer fee than for his exploits for Sunderland. In fact, after signing from South Hylton Club juniors in 1900, Common had done little for the club and he was transferred to Sheffield United in 1902 for £320. Sunderland brought the local lad back home two years later for £520, and for just over half a season Alf Common was a first team regular. Then Middlesbrough, who were struggling at the bottom of Division One, came in with an astonishing offer of £1,000 for the inside right. Sunderland took the money and on 16 February 1905 Alf Common became the first thousand-pound footballer. Both Sunderland and Middlesbrough were criticised in quarters of the game for dragging a fine old athletic team sport through the gutter of filthy lucre. A hundred years later £1,000 would be worth about £50,000.

But none of these fine diversions could mask the fact that Sunderland's league position was slipping, year after year, and that they rarely got past the first round of the FA Cup. In 1907–08, for instance, they escaped relegation by only two points after a late scare which prompted them to win five of their last seven fixtures. Holley and Billy Hogg themselves scored 11 goals in those seven games. The forwards were prolific enough (Holley finished the season with a bag of 23 goals); it was just that the defence gave away almost as many as the team scored. Sunderland in that season became one of the few teams to finish marginally shy of relegation, but with a positive goal average – 78 scored to 75 conceded. In 1907–08, in fact, Sunderland were the second-highest goalscoring team in Division One, after champions Manchester United – but finished in 16th place! On top of all that, the team was knocked out of the first round of the cup that year by non-league New Brompton.

Something had to be done. The last of the famous international defensive trio, Jimmy Watson, had followed Doig and McCombie out of the door in spring 1907. At this point, defence and the half-back line had clearly to be rebuilt from scratch. So the Welsh amateur international goalkeeper Leigh Richmond Roose was bought from Stoke City.

The 30-year-old Roose was one of the last great eccentric amateur footballers to play at the top level; a throw-back to the 1860s and the 1870s and the pre-league dominance of such teams as Corinthians, Old Carthusians and Wanderers FC. He delighted in the individualism of his character and his position, saying of goalkeeping that it was 'good for a man to be alone'. His goal-kicks were prodigious and he had an unnerving habit of bouncing the ball all the way up to the halfway line before releasing it – a habit which eventually persuaded the FA in 1912 to restrict goalkeepers' handling of the ball to their own penalty area. Unfortunately his Sunderland career was cut short. In 1910, when Roose was just 32 years old, he broke a wrist in an accidental clash with Newcastle's Jackie Rutherford. The club's subsequent attempts to give this immensely popular servant a testimonial were over-ruled by the FA on the grounds that Roose (who had a private income) was an amateur. So he got instead an illuminated address from the Mayor of Sunderland, and the thanks of Wearside for saving the club from relegation.

Roose – a brilliantly athletic, instinctive shotsaver – certainly steadied the ship. The goals-conceded column reduced dramatically in size and the club climbed back up the first division table. Roose did not accomplish this alone, of course. A full-back named Albert Milton ('five foot six and a half inches of solid manhood, with thighs like tree-trunks and the courage of a lion') was signed from Barnsley in October 1908. And Harry Low, a half-back, utility forward, and brother of the famous Newcastle centre-half Wilf Low, came from Aberdeen in 1907.

Charlie Thomson, the captain of Scotland as well as Sunderland, and for more than ten years his country's established centre-half, was signed from Heart of Midlothian in May 1908 to do the same job for Sunderland. A big, powerful man, Thomson is widely credited with being one of the first 'stopper' centre-halves, which is to say that he saw his duties as being primarily defensive, dropped in between the two full-backs and taking care of the opposing centre-forward. He would make sporadic foraging bursts forward, controlling his team's forward motion like a puppet-master, pulling long strings and spraying passes about, rather than push forward himself from the centre of midfield (in the way, for instance, his predecessor as captain Johnny Auld used to do). Not until a former Sunderland footballer, Charlie Buchan, helped to introduce the 'stopper' system to Arsenal almost 20 years later did this new reading of the centre-half role become an everyday part of soccer philosophy. But it is almost certain that Buchan was educated by Thomson in the half-dozen seasons the two men played together.

From the day of his signing Thomson was a vital cog in the Sunderland wheel. Some came to look on him as irreplaceable. When Thomson had to miss a couple of games early in December 1910, Sunderland, who had been sitting on top of the league, drew both matches 1–1 and consequently slipped back into the chasing pack. A local journalist commented:

> In looking over the cause we begin to conjecture on the dire possibilities that lie in the prolonged absence of Charles Thomson . . . It would appear that the defence is all at sea when the skipper is not aboard. His presence is not only valuable so far as defence goes, but it is obvious that things go wrong with the attack also when Charles is not aiding in the combination by pushing the ball ahead . . . 'Tis surely the absence of Charles Thomson that makes all the difference in the working of the side.

Jackie Mordue from Sacriston, County Durham, was bought from Woolwich Arsenal in the same month that Charlie Thomson travelled south from Edinburgh, and quickly worked his way into the forward line alongside Hogg, Holley and Arthur Bridgett. Mordue was rated as the best and quickest two-footed forward of his generation. He played for England on both right and left wings and was capable of filling the other three attacking positions with ease. He had deceptively short strides and shuffling gait – which could explode into extraordinary speed over ten yards. In training, the other Sunderland players would place bets on Jackie Mordue being able to beat an opponent, literally with one arm tied behind his back. He had also the added distinction of being the world champion at hand-ball, the traditional north-eastern version of fives.

In 1908–09 Sunderland finished third in the league. They were a long way off the pace, nine points behind the champions. But the season had its other compensations. The most notable of these came on 5 December 1908, when Sunderland visited the ground of the eventual winners of Division One.

Those champions-elect were Newcastle United. The league leaders had suffered a set-back a couple of weeks previously, losing 2–0 at home to Villa, and as a result they dropped five senior players. The team which faced Sunderland on 5 December 1908 was not, on paper, at full strength. But it was used to victory and unaccustomed to conceding many goals – in their previous 15 league games Newcastle had let in only 13.

During the first 45 minutes there was little sign of what was to come. Billy Hogg gave Sunderland the lead early on, but the big Newcastle support – the crowd was estimated at 56,000 – became revived a minute before the break when Charlie Thomson was judged to have handled in the box. The Geordies' new signing, Albert Shepherd, made it 1–1 from the spot.

The Sunderland players nursed a grievance throughout the half-time break that day at St James's Park, because they considered that the ball had struck Thomson's arm outside the penalty area. But that alone cannot explain the miracle of the second 45 minutes. In the teeming rain, shortly after kick-off Holley made it 2–1 to Sunderland. Ten minutes after that Hogg made it 3–1. Holley almost instantly racked up the fourth and Newcastle fell apart. Hogg and Holley completed their hat-tricks; Bridgett got two; and Mordue one to make the score Newcastle United 1, Sunderland 9, with 15 minutes still to play. Sunderland had scored eight goals in less than 30 minutes, five of them coming in one eight-minute spell. Over at Roker Park a sizeable crowd was watching a reserve match. As the first team score was put up on the board the Wearsiders greeted each goal with a loud cheer – until the fifth, when they fell silent, convinced that somebody was playing an elaborate practical joke.

That 9–1 hammering remains the biggest Division One away win on record, Newcastle's biggest home defeat, and Sunderland's biggest league win at home or away. No champions of the Football League have ever received such a mauling in the course of a title-winning season. Newcastle finished that campaign having conceded just 41 goals in 38 games. Almost a quarter of those 41 goals came in just one of those 38 matches, at home to Sunderland on 5 December 1908.

One way and another, those Edwardian derbies with Newcastle were rarely free of incident. In Wearside eyes the Geordies had hijacked Sunderland's rightful role at the top of Division One – and Sunderland were fighting hard to regain the initiative. The atmosphere and spirit were not always unclouded. On 18 September 1909, with both clubs starting the season high in the first division, some of the 35,000 Roker Park crowd burst onto the pitch at the Fulwell end after United had taken the lead. Two mounted policemen appeared, and in the confusion one of their horses was stabbed. The referee refused to allow a normal half-time period, turned the game straight around, and Newcastle went home 2–0 winners.

Sunderland may have been working hard, but it was clear to all – not least to Robert Kyle, Billy Williams and Fred Taylor – that the team was four or five players short of a championship side, and perhaps one truly memorable player short of a great side. Luckily (if it had anything to do with luck) those gaps were filled.

Frank Cuggy, a defensive half-back, was signed locally from Willingham Athletic early in 1909. Cuggy was one of those footballers whose contribution to a unit – in his case the formidable midfield of Cuggy, Thomson and Low – meant that the sum of his parts was greater than the individual himself.

The next significant player who followed Cuggy to Roker Park could not have been more different, either in style or in contribution. He was the genius in the squad, the central jewel in the diadem. He was one of the two or three most brilliant stars ever to shine in the Sunderland firmament.

Charles Buchan was born in 1890 to a couple from Aberdeen. His father had been a colour sergeant in a Highland regiment who, after leaving the army, travelled to London to work as a blacksmith at the Royal Arsenal in Woolwich. All four of the Aberdeen man's sons – three of whom would later play professional football – were subsequently born in the capital, and were brought up among that host of children of working men from the north of England and Scotland who formed and supported the south's first Football League team at the Royal Arsenal. Charles Buchan would later affectionately remember as a 13-year-old seeing Sunderland play Arsenal at the Manor Field in Woolwich – '[that] forward line which included players like Billy Hogg, Jimmy Gemmell, Alf Common and Arthur Bridgett, all great, husky fellows weighing something like 14 stone each.'

Having failed to win a contract from Woolwich Arsenal, Charlie Buchan was enjoying himself in the Southern League with Leyton Orient – but they made no secret of the fact that their talented (if slightly-built) young forward was for sale. On 10 March 1911 Buchan turned up for training and was sent to the manager's office. Sitting there in that office was Bob Kyle.

'How would you like to play for Sunderland in the first division?' asked Kyle. 'You'll get maximum wages and a ten pounds signing-on fee.'

The maximum wage in 1911 was four pounds a week. Buchan was on three pounds a week at Orient, with the promise of a raise.

Ten pounds would be worth about £500 today. Despite not knowing exactly where Sunderland was – 'I knew it was in the north-east somewhere . . . It seemed very far away from home' – Buchan pocketed Bob Kyle's tenner. 'Son,' said Kyle, 'it's very cold up north, so I advise you to get an outfit of thick winter clothes. You'll need them.'

So it was that Charles Buchan's signing-on fee was spent on a new lined overcoat for four guineas (£210 nowadays) and a tweed suit for £2 10s (£125), all of which he had outgrown within months as the slight and slender 20-year-old leaped up to over six feet in height. Buchan's first home game for his new club came a couple of weeks later, when Middlesbrough were beaten 3–1. As Buchan left the field, big Jimmy Gemmell approached his new inside-forward partner and said, 'If you keep playing like that you'll be king of Sunderland.'

Buchan actually took a famously long time to settle, as Sunderland finished once more among the league runners-up. His rapid increase in height without extra weight (he put on three inches in four months) sapped the young man's strength. The crowd got on his back, he asked to be dropped, and only trainer Billy Williams' patience and fortitude kept him with the club. In his first 14 games Buchan scored only once – and that was something of a fluke in a 1–1 home draw with Notts County at the end of the 1910–11 season. Arthur Bridgett sent a corner kick high into the County goalmouth; Buchan shouted 'Right!' and everybody stood still, including the huge Notts goalkeeper Albert Iremonger. Buchan's unopposed header sailed into the unprotected net. It was the kind of goal which, much later, led to the rule-change which insists upon a name being used in calling for the ball.

This same game, incidentally, taught Buchan one of the lessons which are still learnt early by professional footballers. Notts County had a left-back named Montgomery 'a broad-shouldered, thick-set fellow, only about 5'5" in height, but as tough as the most solid British oak.' In Buchan's words: 'The first time I got the ball, I slipped it past him on the outside, darted round him on the inside and finished with a pass to my partner. It was a trick I had seen Jackie Mordue bring off. It worked wonderfully well. But as I came back down the field, Montgomery said in a low voice: "Don't do that again, son." Of course I took no notice. The next time I got the ball, I pushed it past him on the outside but that was as far as I got. He hit me with the full force of his burly frame so hard that I finished up flat on my back only a yard from the fencing surrounding the pitch. It was a perfectly fair shoulder charge that shook every bone in my body. As I slowly crept back onto the field, Montgomery came up and said: "I told you not to do it again.'"

Once Buchan had got over his growing pains and the Sunderland weather, Bob Kyle's new side began to settle down. Some fine-tuning needed still to be done. Some of that work forced itself upon Kyle. Nobody, for instance wanted to get rid of or replace Arthur Bridgett. The left-winger had had a brilliant career with Sunderland, spanning ten seasons, 347 games and 119 goals.

But Bridgett's strong religious convictions eventually caught up with himself and the club. On the Good Friday of 1912 Sunderland – who were sitting in the top half of the table – were scheduled to play Liverpool in a league game. Bridgett would not play football on holy days. So Harry Martin, who had been signed in January from Sutton Junction, made his début on the left flank. Sunderland lost 2–1 on Merseyside, but Martin scored – and the younger man then held onto Bridgett's place in the team. In May Arthur Bridgett was sold to non-league South Shields as player-secretary for £175. Another forward, Jimmy Richardson, was bought from Huddersfield Town just before the start of the 1912–13 season.

The bizarre thing about that 1912–13 season was how very badly Sunderland started the campaign. Even for a side which was traditionally slow off the blocks, this was an abysmal beginning. After their first seven league matches Sunderland were bottom of Division One, having lost five games and drawn two. The talk on Wearside started to be of possible relegation.

What turned the season around so dramatically? It is easy to point to two signings made by Kyle and Williams in the terrible days of early October. The goalkeeper Joe Butler was bought from second division Glossop. Butler, who was short, sturdy and reliable rather than dramatic, certainly helped to stabilise the defence.

But arguably the greater contribution to the remainder of that season came from the other new signing in the October of 1912, the full-back Charlie Gladwin. Gladwin, who came from Blackpool, was a huge figure in all respects (although his habit of forcing his fingers down his own throat to induce sickness before a match – 'it calms the nerves' – was initially worrying to his new colleagues). Standing 6'1" in his stocking feet and weighing 14 stone, he dominated the penalty area. 'When there's a corner kick against us,' Charlie Gladwin would tell his team-mates, 'all clear out of the penalty area – leave it to me.' They did. The wing-halves Cuggy and Low found themselves free from defensive duties and able to push forward with confidence.

Bob Kyle paid £3,000 for Butler and Gladwin, and many people wondered about spending such an enormous sum on a pair of defenders. But they probably won him the league title, and almost the double. The transformation was immediate. The blend of youth and experience, of new players and old, instantly knitted. Sunderland went on a five-game winning streak. Buchan and Mordue started scoring again, but most vitally, Geordie Holley hit peak form. Now almost 30, he set off on a one-man rampage through the first division. On 2 November 1912, when Sunderland visited Bradford City – FA Cup winners of two years earlier, when they had beaten Newcastle United in the final – Holley destroyed the Yorkshiremen single-handedly. Sunderland won 5–1 that day at Valley Parade, and inside-left Holley netted a hat-trick. But it was the manner of his goals as much as anything which demoralised the opposition. According to a team-mate, each one was scored by Holley 'running nearly half the length of the field and coolly dribbling the ball round goalkeeper Jock Ewart before placing it in the net.'

A month after that, with Sunderland now half-way up the table and still going strong, on 7 December 1912 the Wearsiders beat Liverpool 7–0 at Roker Park. Charlie Buchan got five goals that day against Kenny Campbell, Liverpool's Scottish international goalkeeper. 'Four of them,' said Buchan later, 'I just touched into the net. Holley had beaten the defence and even drawn Campbell out of position before giving me the goals on a plate.'

There were glitches, of course. Minor ones – like centre-half and captain Charlie Thomson one day failing to take Gladwin's advice to get out of the area at corner-kick time. Thomson hung around in the danger zone, and Gladwin's inevitable full-bodied clearance struck the elegant Scot full on his black flowing moustache. Thomson – certainly no wilting violet – was brought round in the dressing room and allowed back on the field in the second half (there were no substitutes allowed in 1912). Once back on the pitch, the still-concussed Sunderland captain proceeded to play for the opposition!

There were less minor glitches too, like defeats at Manchester City and West Brom. But the side which this reborn Sunderland team feared above all was Aston Villa, who were themselves aiming for the league and cup double. Wearside hopes were raised on 23 November 1912 when goals from Mordue, Buchan and Holley defeated Villa 3–1 in the league.

The FA Cup campaign, that perennial bugbear to Sunderland, started well for once. Four goals from Richardson helped to see off second division Clapham Orient by 6–0 in the first round. But from then onwards it was a hard, unrelenting cup campaign.

The second round match at Manchester City on 1 February 1913 attracted enormous interest and an equally huge Mancunian crowd. So large was the attendance that people were crammed around the touchline like a human wall, and the moment the game kicked off spectators began to encroach onto the playing area all around the field. Two goals from Buchan gave Sunderland an apparently safe passage into the third round, but with 25 minutes to go the referee had to abandon the tie due to crowd trouble. The Football Association fined City an unprecedented £350 – and ordered the game to be replayed at Roker Park. Luckily, Sunderland made no mistake at home. A penalty from Mordue and another goal from Buchan in open play saw them win 2–0.

In the third round Swindon Town visited Roker Park. Swindon were a non-league club, but this did not signify a walk-over. The Wiltshire team were among the strongest in the Southern League and included the great Harold Fleming, a current England international, brilliant ball-player and deadly striker who scored nine goals for his country in nine games. Nonetheless Sunderland sent Fleming and Swindon home well beaten by 4–2. One of the Wearsiders' winning goals came from the wonderful Charlie Gladwin, his only strike in 62 Sunderland games.

The quarter-final produced the dream draw: Sunderland against Newcastle United. It was the third time the two north-eastern giants had met in the cup. The Geordies had won the two previous ties. But before this one could be settled, it went the full distance, and more.

At Roker Park on 8 March the two teams drew 0–0. They progressed to St James's Park four days later. Holley scored for Sunderland and the teams were drawing 1–1 when, with just a few minutes left, Charlie Buchan headed Sunderland into the lead. As the ball struck the back of the net, Buchan said that he saw 'a vision of the Crystal Palace [where the finals were played] as clear as a picture on the top of the cross-bar'. But with seconds to go Buchan's vision disingrated – Newcastle's skipper Colin Veitch slipped the ball to centre-half Wilf Low and from 30 yards out Harry Low's brother tried a speculative shot. It was going nowhere, until Charlie Gladwin took a wild lunge at the ball. Instead of clearing the half-way line, it careered off Gladwin's boot and past Butler for an equaliser. The score was still 2–2 after extra time.

(Back in Sunderland later that evening the despondent Gladwin boarded a tramcar. He heard a fellow passenger, who was utterly unaware of the proximity of the Sunderland full-back, say out loud: 'I wonder how much Gladwin got for putting the ball through his own goal.' Gladwin smacked the speaker on the chin, toppling him off the tram and leaving him lying, feet in the air, on the road as the vehicle moved away.)

The two managers, Bob Kyle and Frank Watt – two of the greatest football managers the north-east has known – tossed a coin for the venue of the third tie. Watt called correctly and it returned to Newcastle. But this time Sunderland's traditional mastery at St James's Park re-asserted itself before 50,000 fans; goals from Mordue (2) and Holley brought a 3–0 win in a snowstorm.

Neither the weather nor Sunderland's fixture congestion eased up in the semi-final. Burnley, who were fighting (successfully) for promotion from Division Two that season, were drawn at Bramall Lane, Sheffield. In torrential rain, the first match was once more drawn 0–0. But the replay on 2 April 1913 at St Andrew's in Birmingham was a classic cup-tie. Burnley's two stars, the centre-half Tommy Boyle and striker Bert Freeman – both England internationals at the top of their form – appeared to take control of the match, and with 25 minutes to go the Lancastrians were leading 2–1, only a Buchan goal keeping Sunderland in the cup. Then Jackie Mordue converted a penalty kick, and with the minutes ticking away Geordie Holley made it 3–2 for the Wearsiders.

For the first time in their immensely distinguished history, Sunderland were in the cup final! When the players returned to the north-east on Thursday 3 April, the day after the match, they were mobbed by a huge crowd outside the station, and some of them had to hide for two hours in a tobacconist's shop! What was more, they already knew the opposition. The previous Saturday Aston Villa had taken just one game to dismiss Oldham Athletic in the other semi-final.

This was a duel to the end. Villa had hit a superb run of league form and were edging closer to Sunderland at the top. But Sunderland more than matched the midlanders. Between the first Newcastle quarter-final tie on 8 March and the cup final on 19 April, Sunderland played seven league games – and won them all. Nonetheless, the week of the final was incredibly dramatic. Villa and Sunderland met on Saturday 19 April at Crystal Palace in the cup final, and then again just four days later, on 23 April at Villa Park in the league. Those two matches held the key to the double, for both sides.

Sunderland lost one competition and won the other. Few teams came as close to a twentieth century double before Spurs finally achieved it in 1961. The cup final at the Crystal Palace arena in Sydenham was an epic occasion, if not a brilliant match. An astonishing crowd of 120,000 – the biggest ever to watch a football match in England, other than at the first Wembley final in 1923 – turned up to see what were indisputably the best two teams in the country.

Sunderland were the bookies' favourites, but Villa – as marginal underdogs – were the darlings of the huge neutral support. Sunderland had not had the best preparation for their first FA Cup final. Ten days earlier, during a 3–1 home league win over Everton, Geordie Holley had picked up a bad ankle injury. It was decided to rest Holley for the final and play the substitute inside-forward Walter Tinsley instead. But just before the final Tinsley himself fell ill, so an unfit Holley took the field.

It should still have been enough. But somehow the 'Sunderland triangle', the right-flank combination of half-back Frank Cuggy and forwards Mordue and Buchan – a threesome that was described as 'perpetual motion', and all of whom were to be picked in their club positions for England that year – never got going. The defences of both teams took a firm grip on the game, perhaps too firm. Sunderland captain and centre-half Charlie Thomson got into an evil-tempered duel with Villa's intensely physical English international centre-forward Harry Hampton. Two weeks earlier Thomson and Hampton had met in an England v. Scotland match at Stamford Bridge. Hampton had then scored the only 'goal' for his country against Scotland by charging the Scottish goalkeeper, Brownlie – who had the ball in his arms – wholesale into the back of the net. Charlie Thomson's anxiety to prevent the Villa forward from repeating such tactics in the cup final ensured a vicious clash.

Although neither man was sent off, their behaviour during the final was judged by the FA to be so reprehensible that both of them were suspended for a month at the start of the following season.

Shortly after kick-off Charlie Buchan found himself waiting for a throw-in alongside Villa's inside-left Clem Stephenson. 'Charlie,' said Stephenson, 'we're going to beat you by a goal to nothing.'

'What makes you think that?' replied Buchan.

'I dreamed it last night,' said Stephenson. 'Also that Tom Barber's going to score the winning goal.'

The game continued at headlong pace. Villa missed a penalty, then early in the second half Villa's international goalkeeper Sam Hardy was injured. The game was held up for fully seven minutes before Hardy was finally stretchered from the field. Villa continued with ten men, centre-half Jim Harrop going in goal.

Desperate to milk this advantage, Sunderland flung themselves into attack. Twice they hit the post with Harrop beaten – and then, after 20 minutes away, Hardy returned to his post, Harrop went back into defence, Villa pushed back into attack and won a corner out on the right. Charlie Wallace took it, and the ball swung low into the confusion of bruised and tiring players in the Sunderland penalty area. There the Villa right-half Tom Barber dashed forward, stooped, connected with the ball, and sent it flying past a helpless defence and static Joe Butler into the corner of the net.

Clem Stephenson's dream, and Sunderland's nightmare, had come true. At their first attempt, they had lost the FA Cup final by 1–0. A group of members of the Supporters' Club had travelled to London with a crate of specially brewed beer. After the defeat they left the bottles unopened. The beer would be drunk, they said, only when Sunderland won the FA Cup. It was drunk, in time; but it would be extremely mature ale.

There was still the league – and to be sure of that, the tired and dispirited Sunderland players had to avoid defeat by Villa in the midlands four days later. This time Holley was rested, and Walter Tinsley played. Before an immense league crowd of 70,000 at Villa Park, Tinsley scored after ten minutes. Sunderland's defence shut up shop, and although Villa snatched an equaliser in the second period, Sunderland went away with a vital point from a 1–1 draw.

They needed two more points from two remaining games to clinch the title. On Saturday 26 April they got them with a 3–1 win over Bolton Wanderers in Lancashire. Just one record remained to be achieved. In the eight seasons since Division One had been expanded to 20 clubs, no champion had ever won more than 52 points from their 38 games. A Charlie Buchan goal beat Bradford City by 1–0 at Roker Park on 30 April 1913, to give Sunderland the title with 54 points – the most that anybody ever totalled in a 38-game first division campaign.

It was some team, that squad which set off for a celebratory tour of Hungary, Austria and Germany (seven games, seven wins). But it was fragile and doomed, not only by external events – which would be cataclysmic enough – but also by its own inner fault-lines. It was so much a happy mixture of youth and experience that it began to fall apart almost immediately. The youth moved on to pastures new, and the experience either retired or dropped down a level.

Slowly the side dissolved. In doing so, it did not disgrace itself. Sunderland finished seventh and eighth in the league in the two seasons after the 1912–13 championship, and reached the FA Cup quarter-final in 1914. The year tells its own story. Britain entered the First World War shortly before the start of the 1914–15 football season. But the war was expected to be all over by Christmas. Therefore the season was allowed to run its course in a strangely muted atmosphere. And when the season finished, the players went off to the recruiting stations.

Some never returned. Leigh Richmond Roose, the great eccentric amateur goalkeeper, was killed in France in 1916 – a month after the death in action of the Durham man Thomas Sowerby Rowlandson, who briefly kept goal for the club after the departure of Ned Doig in 1904. The wonderful left-back of the 1912–13 championship side, Albert Milton, also perished in the conflict.

Others were more fortunate. The reserve Jimmy Seed returned

from France having been gassed and, as his fitness was suspect, Sunderland transferred him. Seed was eventually picked up by Tottenham, and went on to enjoy a sparkling career. And the rest trickled back in more or less mint condition – not least the remarkable Charlie Buchan, who had managed to get through the killing fields of the Somme, Cambrai and Passchendaele without a scratch.

Between 1915 and 1919 Sunderland AFC played no competitive football at all – the north-east was just too distant from the rest of England for them to compete even in the scratch wartime leagues. The financial burden was consequently so great that one or two important young players were sold – not least the promising half-back Billy Cringan, who went to Celtic in 1915, and later became Scotland's centre-half.

Geordie Holley returned, but would never play a post-war league or cup game. He was transferred to Brighton & Hove Albion before returning to take on the coach's job at Roker Park. Harry Martin came back, along with Buchan and Mordue and Cuggy, and goalkeeper Leslie Scott. And so Sunderland entered the inter-war years.

FIVE

The Nearly Years

1919–1931

The full campaign did not resume until the end of August 1919. In the months beforehand Sunderland re-assembled their players, took stock, and warmed up in a north-eastern 'Victory League' with Newcastle, South Shields, Scotswood and others. Sunderland won it.

That preparation successfully over, and with his club clearly re-established as the top side in the north-east, Bob Kyle slowly reassembled his Football League professional squad. When Sunderland kicked off in peacetime once more, at home to Aston Villa on 30 August 1919, most of his pre-war players were still available. Charlie Buchan in particular, unscathed and the holder of a Military Medal, seemed unaffected by four years of conflict: the number eight got one of Sunderland's goals in a 2–1 win before 35,000 celebrating fans that day.

Buchan had been in fact on the verge of leaving. Chelsea were keen to sign him, and he liked the idea of returning to London. He was packed and ready to go, but shortly before his train for the south was due to leave, Bob Kyle called at the Buchan household with the information that Sunderland 'would never' agree to the transfer. Buchan unpacked – and was given a second testimonial, in recognition of his 'wasted' war years. He then set about reducing his soldier's weight of 15 stone back down to his playing size of just over 13 stone.

They were hard games for all footballers, those first competitive games after the First World War. Nobody was properly fit, nobody was match-trained, and they were playing for just 30 shillings a week maximum in a period of post-war inflation. (The minimum wage would soon have to be raised to the unthinkable sum of ten pounds a week.)

But it was peace, and it was soccer again. The club entered the years between the wars as part of that brawny world of post-Edwardian sport which, in Britain at least, was still insular and eccentric. It was a world in which a pair defenders would approach a skilful forward just before kick-off – as once happened at an away game to a dangerous Sunderland attacker – and one defender would say: 'If you come any of your tricks today, I'll kick you over the grandstand.' Then his team-mate would add: 'And I'll go round the other side and kick you back on the field again.'

This pie-and-bovril game had strong roots still in the old gamesmanship traditions of Victorian sport. In 1919 Colonel Joe Prior became a director. Colonel Joe – who would be chairman of the club between 1940 and 1949 – had inherited his father's Wearside haulage company after returning from the Boer War, and had commanded the Tyneside Irish during the First World War. To such a man, sport was simply sport. He had known more serious things. He announced his arrival at the club by locking a fellow director overnight in the toilet of a Liverpool hotel before an away game on Merseyside. When the club sent Colonel Joe to Glasgow to sign a player, he decided against it and came back with two horses instead. As chairman of the board he became one of the great figures of British sport. During a Sunderland tour of continental Europe, Colonel Joe was observed to spend the whole of a match in Lille sitting in the directors' box in stovepipe trousers and large cravat, shouting merrily 'Vive la France!' – to the great amusement of his hosts – while Sunderland struggled to a 5–3 victory.

As Sunderland settled down to this old familiar world, some of the old squad left and new boys arrived. The formidable Jackie

Mordue left for Middlesbrough before the end of the 1919–20 season. This not only broke up the famous right flank 'triangle' of Cuggy, Mordue and Buchan; it also left Sunderland dangerously exposed in one vital area. Mordue had been a deadly penalty taker. For fully a year and a half after he left, Sunderland failed to convert a single spot kick.

But Mordue had slowed down, as had Frank Cuggy. 'Go home and get a bike!' came the unkind advice from the Roker terraces – and Cuggy followed Mordue. But it was centre-half Charlie Thomson, one of those who did not try to resurrect his career after the war, who would prove the most difficult to replace. As Sunderland stuttered into fifth and then twelfth position in the first two post-war seasons, Bob Kyle worked his way through five different centre-halves.

The manager thought he had found the answer in March 1922, when he paid Hull City a record £5,250 for their Scottish international centre-half Michael Gilhooley. And indeed, during Gilhooley's first four matches the defence – which had been leaking a goal and a half per game – conceded only one goal. But then Micky Gilhooley was injured, and bad fortune dogged the Scotsman; two years after that he broke a leg and his top-class career was over.

It was essentially a new Sunderland which achieved the most successful season of the disappointing 1920s. The Hexham boy Ed Robson took over from Leslie Scott between the sticks. In front of him a north-eastern prodigy, Warneford 'Warney' Cresswell, a right-back who had been capped for England while playing for Second Division South Shields, was bought from the Tyneside club for the small fortune of £5,500. One of those defenders ahead of his time, Cresswell attracted some criticism in the early 1920s for his unusual habit of backing off a forward, inducing the attacker to make a mistake, rather than diving in headlong. He did not stay long at Roker, but while he was there Warney Cresswell made a difference. Alongside Cresswell was his complete opposite as a defender, left-back Ernie England, who became famous for his scything sliding tackles, and who was a scoop from the Derby County youth team.

Add the half-backs Charlie Parker and J.W.F. Kasher, from Seaham Harbour and Crook respectively, both swapping about between centre-half and right-half; Jack Poole at left-half; Billy Ellis holding down the left-wing position; and a new centre-forward, Jock Paterson from Leicester City, assisting Buchan up front – and Sunderland at the start of the 1922–23 season looked at last to have rediscovered their direction.

In fact the season – and the team – flattered to deceive. After the traditional mediocre start Sunderland kicked into gear early in November. They got on the heels of the reigning champions, Liverpool, and between 11 November and 24 February put together a club record sequence of 16 undefeated games – commencing with a 2–0 home win over Newcastle.

Buchan and Paterson were combining irresistibly, with the apparently ageless Buchan netting a personal career best of 30 goals in the season, and Paterson clocking up 21. In the middle of this title-chasing run Charlie Buchan scored probably his most memorable Sunderland goal – a strike which so endeared itself to Wearside that the reporter Arthur Appleton noticed two mentions of it in the same issue of a local newspaper fully 34 years later, in 1957!

It did not come in the league, and it hit the back of the net in a game which Sunderland lost. It came in the second round of the FA Cup, on 3 February 1923, at the ground of West Bromwich Albion. It was, in Buchan's own words, 'one of those goals which come off once in a thousand times'. The ball was crossed in from the left, and it reached inside-right Buchan at knee-height, 25 yards from goal. Charlie checked around him, saw no colleague well-placed for a lay-off, and so 'I took a first-time kick at it . . . The ball simply flew past Hubert Pearson, the Albion goalkeeper, before he could move. It might have gone anywhere. It was the sort of spectacular affair that people remember.'

Albion won that cup tie 2–1, however, despite Buchan's

wondergoal. The player himself preferred one scored against West Brom a few weeks earlier, in a league match at Roker which Sunderland won 3–2, when all the Sunderland front five contributed to a flowing move which left Buchan to tap the ball unspectacularly into an empty net. But it was the cup goal that the local press forever associated with Buchan – and for years afterwards when Charlie visited The Hawthorns, some Albion supporter would approach him to ask: 'Do you remember that goal you scored against Albion in that cup tie here . . ?'

Free from the FA Cup, Sunderland put down their heads and chased Liverpool for the league throughout the early months of 1923. By the middle of February it seemed they might make it. But the defence cracked and the Buchan and Paterson goal machine dried up simultaneously. Thirty-five thousand hopeful Wearsiders turned up for the home game against Sheffield United on 11 April, only to see their club's title hopes disappear in a disastrous 5–3 defeat. 'Unfortunately,' Charlie Buchan would recall, 'we weakened in the final month of the season.' Sunderland lost four of their last six league matches and Liverpool took the title by six clear points. By the time of the last home match, against the usually attractive Aston Villa on 28 April, the league had gone west and only 8,000 fans paid to enter Roker Park. Sunderland finished that promising season with just one title to the club's name: Charlie Buchan's 30 goals were enough to make the England inside-right, at the age of 31 and for the first and only time in his distinguished career, the first division's top scorer.

It was a new Sunderland side, however, and Bob Kyle had reason to hope for better things the following year. Once more the manager went into the market-place. He picked up a new goalkeeper in yet another merciless swoop. Non-league Leyland Motors' 22-year-old keeper, Albert 'the Great' McInroy, had been attracting much attention from top clubs. McInroy's contract with the Lancashire works team ran out at midnight on 6 May 1923. Kyle signed the custodian – reputedly in the toilets of a Manchester hotel – at two minutes past midnight. McInroy was paid £10 in his hand and Leyland Motors got £100. Sunderland had picked up a goalie who would provide them six years' loyal service.

That tricky position plugged, Kyle then collected the Scottish international right-half Billy Clunas from St Mirren. Clunas not only started scoring penalties for the club, thereby filling a gap which had existed since the departure of Jackie Mordue (Clunas would pick up a useful 44 goals in his eight seasons with the club), he also combined with Charlie Parker and Arthur Andrews from Durham City to make up a decent half-back line.

Yet again, Sunderland started the 1923–24 season badly, taking just three points from their first four games. And yet again they picked up in October, embarking on an undefeated run that took the club to within sight of the top of the division. But yet again they lost three of their last five league games – games that would have won them the league, for Sunderland finished third in Division One, four points behind champions Huddersfield Town.

And a year later, in the close season of 1925, after the club had finished in a disappointing seventh position, Sunderland lost their last playing link with that glorious side of the years before the First World War. Charlie Buchan was 33 years old, and understandably expected to finish his career at Roker Park. Only one club in England could have tempted him away – and that club, the Arsenal which he had supported as a boy, did so.

They came straight to his door. Buchan had recently bought out his partner's share in his Sunderland sports outfitters' shop, and was serving behind the counter one day on May 1925 when no less a figure than Herbert Chapman walked in. Chapman had been manager of the Huddersfield team which had frustrated Sunderland two years earlier, and had recently moved to Highbury. 'I've come to sign you on for Arsenal,' he said.

'Shall we go into the back room and sign the forms?' joked Buchan.

'I'm serious,' said Chapman. And he was. Bob Kyle had already given Chapman permission to approach Buchan. A Sunderland director, George Short, resigned over the controversial transfer, but it went ahead. Financially, Sunderland reckoned to have done very well out of it. Arsenal's Sir Henry Norris and Bob Kyle could not agree on a transfer fee. Kyle asked for £4,000. Norris refused. So Kyle suggested £2,000 down, and an extra £100 for every Arsenal goal scored by Buchan during his first season. Kyle was not really gambling: Buchan had averaged 20 goals a season during the post-war years. In his first term at Highbury he scored 19 league goals and two in the FA Cup, which brought the amount paid to Sunderland by Arsenal to £4,100 – just over Kyle's initial asking price.

So ended one of the most fabled of Sunderland careers. During his 11 seasons at the club (divided, of course, by the four wasted years of war) Buchan had got his hands on only one trophy: that of the league in 1912–13, the season that Sunderland had also reached the FA Cup final. But his consistency and skills gave the 'sand-dancer' 224 goals in 413 league and cup appearances. Above all, perhaps, Charlie Buchan was a soccer intellectual, the ultimate in thoughtful inside-forwards. Even while still playing at Sunderland he was writing for the newspapers, and in retirement he would bring the schoolboys of Britain their first truly popular soccer magazine: *Charles Buchan's Football Monthly*. Nor was his playing influence dead once he left Wearside. At Arsenal, in collaboration with the great Herbert Chapman, Buchan is credited with introducing the truly defensive centre-half system, bringing that player back between the full-backs rather than leaving him to roam midfield, thereby stemming the rush of goals which had followed the recent amendment of the offside law. (The law change now meant that only two, rather than three, players had to be between the attacking team and the goal.)

The Sunderland fans' obvious disappointment at the loss of their most famous player was quickly eased by the start of the 1925–26 season. They got off to their best start in history, winning their first four matches on the trot, scoring 20 goals for the loss of six, and going straight to the top of Division One. Perhaps most promisingly, fully ten of those 20 goals in four games were scored by a new signing, the tall, elegant, left-footed Scottish centre-forward David Halliday, who had been bought in from Dundee before Buchan's transfer.

Halliday did not stop scoring. He finished the season with 38 league goals and four in the cup. But his defence let him down. He was capable of netting five goals in four games during the crucial mid-season period – only to see those games result in three draws and a defeat. And once again Sunderland had to settle for third place in the league, a long way behind champions Huddersfield and – more gallingly – Charlie Buchan's new club, runners-up Arsenal.

In fact, Arsenal and Buchan would blame Sunderland for costing them the chance of the title, in a strangely bad-tempered and eventful fixture that left its mark on both Wearside's new and old heroes. Buchan had to wait almost a whole season for his return to Roker Park as an Arsenal player – the league game was not scheduled until 10 April, the third-last match of the season.

By that time Sunderland were effectively out of the title race. But Arsenal, who had just beaten leaders Huddersfield, were still in it when they travelled to the north-east. Buchan got, as he may have expected, a wonderful reception from the Roker crowd. Then, just a few minutes into the match, came a peculiar incident. The new centre-forward Dave Halliday – normally the most easy-going of footballers – got into a fracas with Arsenal goalkeeper Dan Lewis. Both men were sent off. As they walked, one after the other, from the Fulwell End to the changing rooms, 'a stunned silence of disbelief' settled on the ground, according to the eyewitness Arthur Appleton, who would later say that he had 'witnessed no ordering-off as shocking'.

As Arsenal captain, Charlie Buchan had to pick up the pieces. In those days before substitutes were allowed, he had no option but to put an outfield player in goal. He decided on the young and speedy outside-right, Joe Hulme. It was a mistake. Hulme would become celebrated as a forward – he was not long afterwards capped by England – but he was no goalkeeper. Shortly after he took over in goal a popular recent Sunderland signing – a player who was many years later to achieve what no previous Sunderland footballer had ever achieved – gave the Wearsiders the lead.

Inside-left Bobby Gurney came from Silksworth and had played for Hetton Juniors and Bishop Auckland before Bob Kyle knocked on his door. The Arsenal home game on 10 April 1926 was only his fourth match in a Sunderland shirt. He watched Lewis leave the field, saw Hulme take his place, and shortly afterwards curled a testing cross-cum-shot into the box. Hulme failed the test: the ball swerved over his flailing arms and into the net. Gurney got another one to seal a 2–1 win – but the drama was not over. Shortly before the end Charlie Buchan went for a cross in competition with his former team-mate, Sunderland centre-half Charlie Parker. Parker fell awkwardly and stayed down. He recovered enough to play on, but the crowd turned against Buchan. This man, who had walked onto the field to warm applause, walked off it 100 minutes later to boos and catcalls, with a feeling of genuine puzzlement – Buchan had not only seen his new club's championship hopes evaporate on his former home turf, but into the bargain he was now being jeered for the kind of challenge that the crowd had enjoyed in a Sunderland shirt. For a man who still half-considered Wearside as his home (and who had actually attempted to get transferred back to Sunderland), it was a disappointing day.

Halliday recovered from his dismissal. He served a suspension at the start of the following season – but scored a hat-trick on his return, in a 7–1 home win over Burnley, and went on to net an astonishing 35 league goals in 33 matches, helping to make Sunderland, with a grand total of 98, the top scoring side in Division One in 1926–27. But it was still not enough to regain the title. Once again Sunderland finished in third place, behind Huddersfield and – more painfully – champions Newcastle United.

The following season, 1927–28, saw the drama take place at the other end of the table. It was most unwelcome, utterly unexpected, and it all came about in the last half-dozen matches.

Sunderland had been playing poorly and were resigned to a

place in the bottom half of the table. But they did not anticipate what was to come. By the middle of April some eight teams were jostling to avoid the two relegation places. Sunderland were marginally above the danger zone. But they then lost four matches in succession. The last of these, at home to a Sheffield Wednesday team inspired by former Sunderland player Jimmy Seed, saw Wednesday seize a 3–2 win and haul themselves to safety. But that result put Sunderland second from bottom – in a relegation place – with just one game left. And that game was away against Middlesbrough, who had the same points but a better goal-average.

Simply, on 5 May 1928 Sunderland needed to win at Ayresome Park to stay up; but thanks to their goal-average a draw would have kept Middlesbrough safe. Aside from their terrible run of form, Sunderland were hampered by injuries. Albert McInroy had missed the Wednesday game and under normal circumstances would have been unfit to play. But trainer Billy Williams strapped the goalkeeper up and sent him out. It was to prove an inspired decision.

Middlesbrough attacked like furies throughout the first half of that momentous game. But McInroy and full-backs Ernie England and Bill Murray (a recent signing from Cowdenbeath) played out of their skins to keep the game goalless until just before half-time. Just then inside-right Billy Wright, who had arrived at Roker alongside Murray from Cowdenbeath, slid in to put Sunderland 1–0 ahead. After the break Middlesbrough collapsed. Halliday made it 2–0 and outside-left Billy Death wrapped it up with a third. A 15-year-old Sunderland supporter would later remember watching that game 'with breathless excitement'. His name was Horatio Carter, and he was known to his family and friends as Raich.

So, just one season after promotion, Middlesbrough went back down and Sunderland stayed up. So close were things at the bottom that, with that one victory, the Wearsiders sat six places clear of relegation, but just one point off the bottom two!

That heartstopping match at Ayresome Park marked the last

game of manager Bob Kyle and trainer Billy Williams – the most consistent managerial combination in the club's history. Kyle had been around since 1905 and had guided at least three separate generations of great sides in his 23 years. Williams had been at Roker for even longer, since before the ground was opened in the late 1890s. An era passed with those two giants; a link with the birth of organised soccer in England. No greater tribute could be paid to Kyle and Williams than that these two footballing men, born and raised in the distant sporting world of the Victorian century, had managed to keep Sunderland Football Club at the pinnacle of competitive soccer well into the modern era.

They were replaced by another manager-trainer team: Johnny Cochrane and Andy Reid from St Mirren. It would be left to Cochrane to capture, in the twentieth century, the one trophy which had eluded his predecessors.

Cochrane and Reid, ably assisted by their Scottish scout Sammy Blyth, built their new team slowly and modestly. In their first season Sunderland finished fourth, thanks largely to the miraculous goalscoring feats of Dave Halliday, who managed 43 goals in 42 league games to finish up as Division One's top scorer. Halliday's accomplishment would have attracted much more attention at the time if he had not been born into a period of record-breaking strikers – the previous season Everton's Dixie Dean had topped the goalscoring table with an unbelievable 60 league goals; and 12 months before that Middlesbrough's George Camsell had notched up 59 in the Second Division!

But it was Halliday's swansong at Roker Park. Just 11 games into the next season, on 29 November 1929, the tall, graceful centre-forward was sold to Arsenal for £6,000. It had been an incredible club career. Dave Halliday managed 162 goals in 175 league and cup matches – an extraordinary 0.92 goals per game. And throughout all those glittering seasons during which he was Sunderland's (and the Football League's) top goalscorer, he was never once capped for Scotland.

Sunderland had gone for the money. They had no immediate

replacement for big Dave. Bobby Gurney stood in at centre-forward for a game or two; Paddy Gallacher arrived from Celtic to bolster the forward line; and in the following close season the left-winger Jimmy Connor was bought from St Mirren to commence one of the most popular of Roker careers. Left-half Alex Hastings appeared from Stenhousemuir. But Sunderland paid for the absence of Halliday with several years of league mediocrity: their average goal haul dipped by up to 20 goals a season and they seemed firmly anchored in mid-table.

There was a hint of what was to come in 1931, when Cochrane's Sunderland reached the semi-finals of the FA Cup for the first time since before the First World War, but in a game of missed opportunities they were knocked out 2–0 by Birmingham at Elland Road. There followed several signings. Three of them would prove extremely significant. The right-winger Bert Davis was bought from Bradford Park Avenue. A brilliant 17-year-old goalkeeper, Jimmy Thorpe, was signed from Jarrow. And on 12 November 1931 an equally young inside-forward was picked up from the local works team, Sunderland Forge.

SIX

Two Horatios and the FA Cup

1931–1939

Horatio Stratton Carter was a well-known local junior footballer. The son of a former professional, 'Toddler' Carter of Port Vale, Fulham and Southampton, 'Raich' Carter himself – who had been born in Sunderland in 1913 and was a pupil of Hendon Boys School, close by the club's old ground – was picked for Sunderland Boys, Durham County, and later England Schoolboys. Leicester City had had their eyes on this infant prodigy for years – some said since Raich was three years old and a Leicester scout met him at his father's home!

In fact, when he was just 14 years old and about to leave school in 1928, Carter was approached by the new Sunderland boss Johnny Cochrane and asked to sign amateur forms, leading to full professional status on his seventeenth birthday. Raich was 'thrilled and eager to do so', but his uncle, a future Deputy Chief Constable of Sunderland who had looked over the lad since the early death of his father, intervened. 'Get a trade', said this policeman, and so Raich Carter became an apprentice electrical engineer with the Sunderland Forge and Electrical Company, for whose works team he played football.

On 21 December 1930 Raich had his seventeenth birthday. Four days later, on Christmas Day, Sunderland were at home to Leicester City. Carter went along to Roker Park, watched Leicester beat

Sunderland by 5–2, and then sought out that old friend of his family, the Leicester scout George Metcalfe. Metcalfe introduced the teenager to the Leicester team and arranged him a trial outing for the City Reserves three days later.

Luckily, the Filbert Street ground was a quagmire after three games in as many days in terrible December weather – and young Raich was picked on the left wing, a position which he hated. A small, slight boy who in his prime stood just 5'8" tall, and who at 17 was much shorter than that, Carter got lost in the mud. He missed a number of sitters, and was ignored by his team-mates for most of the second half.

'Son,' said the Leicester manager afterwards, 'you're too small to play football. Go home.'

So Raich Carter returned to the Sunderland Forge and Electrical Company. And Leicester City missed signing the man whom Charlie Buchan would describe as 'the best forward of his generation'.

And even his home town team took their time. Johnny Cochrane signed Carter on amateur forms and gave him a run-out in a junior team game at the start of the 1931–32 season; but once again Raich fluffed it. It was frustrating, not least because his young career was uncannily echoed by a namesake.

James Horatio Thorpe not only shared an unusual middle name with Horatio Carter. He also was a north-easterner. He also had been born in 1913. And he also had worked as an apprentice engineer – in the Jarrow shipyards. But the 17-year-old goalkeeper, whose career was to end in the most tragic of circumstances, had been given a first-team game almost immediately after signing, and by the end of 1931 he was holding down a Division One place.

In contrast Raich Carter was obliged while signed as a teenaged amateur for Sunderland, to seek first team football with Northern Amateur League club Esh Winning. While there he was approached by a scout from Huddersfield Town. Once more, Carter was almost lost to Wearside. He went to see Johnny Cochrane and asked to be released. Cochrane was a small man with a big temper. He erupted; bawled out Carter; and promptly telephoned Huddersfield's manager Clem Stephenson to accuse him of poaching. While the telephonic battle was raging Carter, having realised that release would not be easy, slunk out of the manager's office.

There was a positive result. Cochrane had been obliged to take notice of his young amateur forward once more, and Raich got selected for the second team in a North-Eastern League match. This time the boy performed well. He was given another reserve outing, and on 12 November 1931 Johnny Cochrane called Raich Carter and his guardian, the policeman uncle, into the manager's office. Carter was offered three pounds a week, with an extra four pounds every time he played for the reserves. This time his uncle approved – the great depression was beginning to bite in the north-east and jobs as electrical engineers did not look so secure as before. Johnny Cochrane counted ten one-pound notes into Carter's hand as a signing on fee, and Raich walked home shortly before his eighteenth birthday as a professional footballer. He certainly did not guess it at the time, but Cochrane had just put into place the cornerstone of one of the greatest and most successful of Sunderland sides.

Life for an apprentice professional in the early 1930s was very different to that of 60 or 70 years later. To begin with, it was not always a full-time job. Carter did not at first give up work at Sunderland Forge. The firm gave him leave for training on Tuesday and Thursday nights – which meant 'doing a work-out in the gym because it was too dark for field work'. On top of that Carter had to attend apprentice's night-classes.

So a month before the 1932–33 season opened, the 18-year-old Carter, determined to get a first-team place as quickly as possible, left the Forge and reported for full-time training at Roker Park. This schedule committed him to training for six days a week, and occasionally on Sundays as well. Once the season started Sunderland players trained twice a day other than match days – which was regarded by some other clubs as excessive. Newcastle

United and Arsenal, for example, at that time trained only once a day. But Cochrane was a strict disciplinarian. He was determined that his players' perceived lack of fitness should not deflect him from his task of winning back his club's lost prestige.

By the start of the 1932 season Carter was fit – fitter than he had ever been – and ready to go. The next obstacle was the pre-season practice matches between first-team and reserve footballers. Like the other second-team men, Carter 'went flat out' to earn his selection, as he would recall:

> That is always the way in these practice games. The reserves are fighting with everything they've got for their big chance, while the concern of the league men is to take it as easily as possible and avoid injuries. I know that as a result of that game I was a bit nervous about showing my face at Roker Park on the following Monday morning. I thought several of the first team players might have been quite outspoken about the way in which I had played in a 'friendly' practice match. But nothing was said. Doubtless they too had done the same in their turn.

On 1 October 1932 Carter edged one step further to a first team début. Sunderland were away at Blackburn Rovers, and Raich was listed as 12th man. He travelled to Lancashire as official reserve and roomed with Paddy Gallacher – the left-sided forward whom Carter hoped to replace. He did not get a game and Gallacher scored all three of Sunderland's goals in a 3–1 win. The last one in particular was utterly memorable and depressing for a reserve. Gallacher received a pass out on the left. With Blackburn's full-back and goalkeeper both rushing out, Paddy executed a neat side-step and dummy – and the two Rovers men collided with each other, fell over, and Gallacher walked round their prostrate forms to roll the ball gently into the open goal.

But two weeks later Gallacher was injured, giving Carter his first-team chance. It was nerve-wracking and he was relieved to hear, as he took his inside-left position just before kick-off, the reassuring tones of left-half Joe Devine behind him saying: 'There's nothing to bother about son. You'll be okay. I'll be right behind you, backing you up.'

Sunderland lost that game, but Carter was picked again the following Saturday, away at Middlesbrough, and this time Sunderland won 2–1. A week later Paddy Gallacher was fit again – but he was picked at inside-right for the home game against Bolton Wanderers. Raich Carter stayed at inside-left.

It was a sensational match, which Sunderland won 7–4. Most fans went home celebrating four goals from centre-forward Bobby Gurney. But at least one young man would remember, most of all, the third goal. Sunderland won a free-kick 25 yards out. Joe Devine took it and passed directly to Raich Carter on the edge of the penalty area. Carter feinted as if to cross with his left foot, then suddenly shifted his weight and shot for goal. The ball flew into the far corner. It would be the first of many. Soon afterwards Carter's weekly wage was raised to eight pounds – the maximum permitted by the Football Association.

Johnny Cochrane had put together a good squad. There was the big-hearted captain and centre-half Jock McDougall from Airdrieonians. There were his fellow half-backs Sandy McNab, who fancied himself as a tap-dancer and would illustrate this skill in the changing room before kick-off (when he was not hosing ice-cold water onto team-mates), and Charlie Thomson, who preferred to prepare for a game by heading a small rubber ball against the wall 300 times without a break.

There was Paddy Gallacher talking tactics in his sleep, young Jimmy Thorpe in goal, and Jimmy Connor out on the left wing – Connor of the astonishing ball control, who once took the ball up to the corner flag and then, instead of crossing, dribbled it all the way along the by-line to the penalty area, beating five panicked defenders in the process, before laying on a tap-in for a colleague.

There was good-natured banter between the Scots and the English – who divided fairly neatly down the middle of

Sunderland's 1930s squad – the keeping tally of goals scored by the different nationalities, and consequent cheerful mockery. And there was another divide, between the older men such as McDougall and the future manager, full-back Bill Murray; and the youngsters like Carter, Thorpe and Gurney, with the inevitable resultant jokes about nappy-changing and nursemaids. It was a fine team to play in. It gave the fans some extraordinary entertainment. Nobody who was there would ever forget the two sixth round FA Cup games against Derby County on 4 and 8 March 1933. The first tie at the Baseball Ground saw Bobby Gurney give Sunderland the lead straight from kick-off, but a see-saw contest swung each way, with six goals scored in the first 35 minutes and the score 3–3 at half-time. Gurney made it 4–3 immediately after the restart, and that was the way it stayed until the very last minute, when Derby's Dally Duncan swerved the ball in from the wing past Jimmy Thorpe.

The replay at Roker Park four days later bore witness to the great longing on Wearside for cup success. An astonishing 75,118 people crammed into the ground that Wednesday night. It was not only Sunderland's record gate; it remains to this day the biggest crowd ever to watch a football match in the north-east of England. (The two home league games on either side of that cup tie attracted just 7,000 and 10,000 paying customers.)

Even after ground expansion, that 75,000 was 10,000 over Roker Park's official capacity of 65,000. The occasion was so immense that it was at best uncomfortable for fans and players alike – and some spectators found the experience positively terrifying. The crowd spilled onto the cinder track around the pitch, and actually squatted on the grass itself. Wingers had to burrow a tunnel through the packed bodies in order to take a corner; half-backs took throw-ins with spectators sitting at their feet. One young fan started watching the match high up on the terracing at the Roker end, and finished it just an inch or two from the touch-line! Several players believed that the game should never have been played – and the Sunderland squad certainly felt uneasy afterwards, for Derby won the replay 1–0 with a Peter Ramage header in extra time.

Exciting as it all may have been, thrilling as the team undoubtedly was, in the cold light of day it was inescapable that Sunderland kept getting knocked out of the FA Cup and finishing in the middle of the Division One table.

Until the season 1934–35. That year certainly repeated the club's traditional heroic failure in the cup. This time it was Everton who helped lay on the thrills in the fourth round. After a 1–1 draw at Roker the two sides met again at Goodison Park. There Everton were leading 3–2 into the last minute, when Bobby Gurney once more stepped into the breach to equalise with a dazzling overhead kick. Sadly, Everton went on to win 6–4 in extra time.

The difference was that following this cup dismissal in January 1935, Sunderland put up a strong challenge for the league title. They were beaten only by a superb Arsenal squad – the new team of Herbert Chapman – which was winning its third consecutive title, scoring a sensational 115 goals in the process. Sunderland had in fact a good record in head-to-head meetings with the Highbury squad. During the Gunners' first title challenge of the hat-trick, in January 1933, Cochrane's side had won a superb league game at Roker by 3–2, coming from 2–1 behind to equalise through Paddy Gallacher, and snatching a dramatic last-minute winner when Raich Carter – dropping back to cover for the tall Alec Hastings, who went forward for a late corner – found the ball bobbling in front of him outside the penalty area and smacked it first time into the net.

In none of their three title seasons did Arsenal manage to win in Sunderland, and it was in clear tribute to their closest challengers that, having completed the hat-trick of championships (and incidentally, having failed in a bid to get Raich Carter to follow in the footsteps of Buchan and Halliday and transfer from Sunderland to north London), Arsenal invited the Sunderland squad to their celebration dinner. Sunderland travelled south especially for that function in the early summer of 1935. They sat in London's

Holborn Restaurant and watched the Arsenal squad receive their championship medals and benefit cheques. They looked enviously at Alex James, David Jack, Ted Drake, Cliff 'Boy' Bastin and the rest of that glamorous, expensive line-up. And they thought, *us next*.

Johnny Cochrane had followed a policy of gradual building, and by the autumn of 1935 his contruction was complete. Jimmy Thorpe, at 21 years old, was judged finally ready to become a permanent fixture between the posts. In front of him was the experienced Bill Murray and Alex Hall, who had arrived from Dunfermline in 1929 but had only lately been able to hold down a regular first team full-back job.

Little Charlie Thomson (he was under 10 stone) and 'non-stop' Sandy McNab – the tap-dance king – vied for the half-back slots with captain and Scottish international Alex Hastings. Jimmy Clarke was signed from Clydebank to compete for the centre-half slot with Bert Johnston – who had in his turn replaced Jock McDougall.

The forward line almost picked itself. Bert Davis had been a fixture on the right wing since arriving from Bradford four years earlier. In the close season of 1933 Len Duns was snatched from Tyneside – from under the very nose of Newcastle United, in fact, as Duns played for one of their founding clubs, Newcastle West End – to challenge Davis and finally take over his right-wing role in what would be a long and very happy Wearside career. Raich Carter, although naturally left-footed, was cleverly picked by Cochrane at inside-right. As Carter had a tendency to drift leftwards onto his favoured foot, this meant that the youngster now drifted towards rather than away from goal – which assisted his natural goalscoring potential. Bobby Gurney had made the number nine shirt his own; Paddy Gallacher was one of the best inside-lefts in the business; and out on the left wing Jimmy Connor was capable of the most astonishing feats of wizardry.

So they won the league. As simple as that – it was a brilliant squad of highly gifted individuals, with a sensational forward line, a backbone of steel, a clever and extremely motivated manager, and a magnificent home support. They were easily the best side in England, and certainly the best Sunderland team since 1913.

They won it easily. Second-placed Derby County finished eight points behind Sunderland in 1935–36, in the days when only two points were given for a win. Sunderland won 25 league games to Derby's 18. Sunderland scored almost twice as many goals as Derby – 109, to County's 61. That was the crux of the matter, as some of the title-winning side would in later years never tire of pointing out. The Sunderland championship team of 1935–36 was an attacking animal, pure and simple. Brilliant to watch, sensational to support. As British football in future years crept into a dull and orthodox defensive shell, those players would look at their own glory days and indicate the huge rise in popular support for the game in the 1930s, and point out: 'We let in more than 70 goals in winning the title, but we scored well over 100. And the crowds loved it!'

Sunderland were excessively, piratically, attacking not only by the standards of later years. They also made most of their 1930s Division One contemporaries look like Arsenal FC under George Graham. No other team in the top half of the division let in 74 goals. You had to make your way down to Wolverhampton Wanderers in 15th position to find a 'worse' defensive record! Liverpool, who escaped relegation by a whisker and who finished 19th, conceded only 64 – ten fewer than champions Sunderland! All of which meant that a customer who coughed up his or her 1/6 to go and see Sunderland play football in the middle of the 1930s was, in any given game, likely to see almost four and a half goals in the average 90 minutes.

This was the final block in the foundations of Sunderland AFC's love affair with Wearside. The 1930s were years of terrible depression in the north-east of England. The poverty of the area was such that visitors even from other parts of the north of England were appalled. When goalkeeper Jimmy Mapson, who had been born on Merseyside, arrived in Sunderland for the first time in 1936, 'It rather shocked me to see kids running about with no shoes on. There was a lot of unemployment about.' And yet this district – apparently written off by the rest of the country – was putting out a football team which not only dominated the best that London and the rest could put out; it also did it in exuberant, exhilarating style. Somehow, conceding those 74 goals was almost as important as scoring the 109. Arsenal had won the title a year earlier by scoring 115 and conceding only 46. But Sunderland – well, Sunderland could afford to give the opposition almost two goals a game, and still win the league by eight clear points!

Of those 109 league goals, Carter, Gurney and Gallacher shared no fewer than 81 – Raich and Bobby getting 31 apiece, and Paddy Gallacher collecting 19.

It was a perfect striker and inside-forward trio, assisted by two dashing wingers and an engine room of intelligent half-backs. They lost their first match, away to Arsenal, and then they took Sunderland straight to the top of Division One by collecting 11 of the next 12 available points. They stumbled a little in late September and early October, but then settled down once more to playing truly championship football. Between 19 October and 14 December they won seven league games, drew one, and lost none.

Sunderland's old inside forward Charlie Buchan caught up with his former club in his new role as a journalist in the middle of this undefeated run. On 16 November he went over to Griffin Park to watch them play Brentford. It was a tricky fixture. Brentford were newly promoted from Division Two, were playing some good football (they would finish in a very respectable fifth position) and like all clubs arriving in the top flight for the very first time, they intended to make an impression. What was more, the afternoon of 16 November 1935 was wet and cold and the ground was rain-soaked.

Buchan need not have worried for his old club. In a season of 'delightful exhibitions' this turned out to be one of the best. Duns, Carter, Gurney (2) and Gallacher shared the goals in a 5–1 win. 'I cannot hope to see anything finer,' wrote Buchan, who continued:

The forward line – Len Duns, Raich Carter, Bobby Gurney, Paddy Gallacher and Jimmy Connor – made the ball do everything but talk. And the defenders, marshalled by Scotland right-back Bill Murray,[1] were as safe as the Bank of England.

'Some people compared them with the 'Team Of All The Talents' way back in the early years of the century, others to the 1912–13 team which nearly brought off the double, winning the league championship but beaten in the FA Cup final by Aston Villa. Well, I cannot write about the early Sunderland. I can about the 1913 team, as I played in it, and I must admit that there was little between the two teams except physique. The 1913 team was much bigger and stronger, but I think the 1936 team almost atoned by their supreme skill and combination. Raich Carter, the silver-haired, local-born inside-right, was the inspiration of the attack. His wonderful positional sense and beautifully timed passes made him, in my opinion, the best forward of his generation . . . He was that rare combination of ball artist and marksman.

By Christmas they had the title virtually sewn up. As Buchan pointed out from the press-box, Raich Carter was on outstanding form, scoring 24 goals in the first 22 matches. The Christmas holiday programme, however, presented three difficult obstacles. Between 21 and 28 December second-placed Derby County, followed by Leeds United and Arsenal, would all visit Roker Park.

Sunderland dismissed them all. Derby were beaten 3–1, Leeds 2–1, and on 28 December 1935, before 59,250 fans, the mighty Arsenal were defeated 5–4 in what one veteran observer described as 'one of the finest games I have ever seen'.

By the middle of April, with four fixtures left, Sunderland

---

[1] Murray made 21 league appearances that championship season – his last in a red and white shirt – but the Brentford away game was not one of them; Buchan was clearly thinking of the full-back's broader contribution.

needed just to win one more game to regain the league title and equal Aston Villa's record of six championships. On the evening of Monday 13 April they visited Birmingham for the first of those last four matches. The midlanders never stood a chance. Gurney hit four goals – one of ten hat-tricks – and Carter, Connor and the reserve forward Cyril Hornby got the others in a 7–2 thrashing. On the following Saturday, 18 April, after an irrelevant 4–3 defeat of Huddersfield Town, the league trophy was presented to captain Alex Hastings on the Roker Park pitch in front of 25,000 fans.

By the time that treasured cup returned to Wearside the club had experienced three traumatic experiences in the second half of their championship season. The first of them was something which the supporters had come almost to expect – although not to such a painful degree.

In the third round of the FA Cup Sunderland were drawn at home to Port Vale. The importance of this venerable trophy to Wearside supporters could not be overstated. It had of course never been won by Sunderland, on any of the previous occasions when they had the best team in England. And with every season that went by without the FA Cup returning to Roker Park, the desperation of fans, players and management alike increased. Attendances for FA Cup games were always enormous; far larger than for league fixtures of comparative importance. 'The Cup was the great prize,' admitted Charlie Buchan. 'Before each season started we heard: 'This is to be Sunderland's year for winning the FA Cup.' Each year the good folk at Sunderland were disappointed . . .'

And so the third round (Sunderland's point of entry) of the FA Cup came around in January 1936, and once more Sunderland sat in their proper place, atop the English First Division, with unarguably the best squad in the country. And they were to play – at home – Port Vale, who were not among the giants of the game in 1936. When Sunderland played them that January, this lowly Potteries club sat uncomfortably at the bottom of Division Two. They would remain there until the season's end, when they were relegated to Division Three (North).

By contrast, Sunderland's 1–0 win over Manchester City at Maine Road on the Saturday before the third round had put them fully seven points clear of Derby at the top of Division One. In that league season Sunderland would score 109 goals in Division One; Port Vale would concede 106 goals in Division Two. This, surely, was a hurdle that even the notoriously cup-shy Sunderland AFC could not fail to clear. But fail they did. Raich Carter would muse on this game many years later:

> With the small clubs a cup-tie is invariably a 'do-or-die' affair. It is their big chance of the season, and they don't give a thought to injuries, which are always the worry of League clubs, particularly those in running for the championship . . . The small club knows that it is not expected to win, and no-one is going to think any the worse of it if it doesn't. The major club, knowing that it *is* expected to win and that to lose will be also a loss of prestige, is more liable to nerves at the start.

Besides, Sunderland were about to become one of the two most successful outfits in English Football League history and the only club in England never to have left Division One (for Aston Villa and Blackburn Rovers were relegated at the end of the season). But for all of their unique accomplishments, they had never won the FA Cup. Add that little weight to the shoulders of Sunderland's footballers and see how they stoop!

Port Vale drew 2–2 at Roker Park in front of a desperate crowd of 30,000 north-easterners. On the following Monday afternoon, 13 January 1936, Sunderland travelled to the Recreation Ground, Hanley, for the replay. The severe frosts in the midlands had rendered an already hard and uneven playing surface both dangerous and difficult. One player split his chin open on the diamond-hard pitch minutes after kick-off, and top-level football became 'just as impossible as good snooker would be on a cracked and unequal billiards table . . . We were reduced to the level of Port

Vale – but with this difference. Port Vale had everything to gain and nothing to lose.'

Tackling and chasing the ball 'with reckless abandon', Port Vale knocked the champions-elect out of the FA Cup by 2–0. That evening, directly after the match, the players and officials of Sunderland AFC returned directly to their training facilities at Hexham. After a tortuous work-out they were allowed back to their hotel at midnight. The players were then allowed a meal. As they pushed back their chairs afterwards and began a weary climb to bed, Johnny Cochrane announced that an inquest would be held at once. These post-mortems were a ritual of Cochrane's, especially after a defeat. He would talk his players through virtually every move in the match and look closely at mistakes.

'What happened just before Port Vale scored their first goal?' Johnny Cochrane asked left-back Alex Hall at approximately 1 a.m. on Tuesday, 14 January 1936.

'I don't know,' replied Hall wearily. 'I gave the ball to Paddy Gallacher.'

Cochrane turned to Gallacher. 'And what happened then?' he demanded.

'I never received it,' said Paddy, and then quickly thought to cover for his team-mate – 'but I think it was a darned good pass all the same!'

The second disruption of Sunderland's road to their sixth title was far more damaging in its implications, and infinitely more tragic. It had been well known at the club that James Horatio Thorpe was diabetic, since he was first diagnosed and started insulin treatment at the local infirmary in 1933. Normally a big, strong man, the 22-year-old goalkeeper had obviously lost a lot of weight over the previous year. 'He seemed to be literally shrinking within himself,' observed one team-mate. Nonetheless Thorpe's performances seemed to be unaffected. For a couple of years between 1933 and 1935 he had effectively shared the keeper's jersey with Matt Middleton, but in the autumn of 1935 Johnny Cochrane made up his mind between the two of them, and

Thorpe became literally the first name to go down on his team-sheet.

On 1 February 1936 Chelsea arrived at Roker for a league game. It was an important match. Sunderland were on top of the league, but the Londoners were by no means out of the title hunt. In an era noted for its robust football matches, this one turned out to be so physical that one Chelsea player was sent off and the crowd turned on both the referee (Mr R.S. Warr of Bolton had to be smuggled out of Sunderland to escape being thrown in the Wear – *before* the last tragic news of this awful match was known) and the Chelsea team. Despite having very little of the game and conceding goals from Bobby Gurney (2) and Paddy Gallacher, Chelsea managed to get a 3–3 draw.

Jimmy Thorpe was the subject of most of the Chelsea intimidation. At that time goalkeepers were offered no special protection by the laws of the game. They were vulnerable to all of the physical challenges which applied outside the penalty area – the celebrated 'shoulder charge' being only one of them. Of course, this meant that goalkeepers were particularly prone to injurious assault, if only because, whereas an outfield player was expected to release the ball and thereby redirect an opponent's challenge, the very nature of the goalie's job insisted that he stand his ground and take both the ball and his punishment. He could not skip away from danger.

A number of well-publicised incidents – such as Manchester City's Bert Trautmann playing through most of an FA Cup final with a broken neck, and Glasgow Celtic's John Thomson dying on the evening of a match as the result of a challenge – eventually led to protective legislation. Firstly, opponents were forbidden to kick the ball when the goalkeeper had it in his hands (a hangover from the old days of football as a semi-handling game, which evolved separately into the code of rugby, and whose last survival in the game of association football is the unique role of the goalkeeper himself). Then the shoulder charge on keepers was outlawed and the modern convention gradually appeared, of the goalkeeper being the single player in a football team upon whom virtually no physical challenge can be mounted. But things were very different in 1936. When Jimmy Thorpe took his position between the posts at Roker Park on 1 February 1936 he was – as he had been throughout his career – a marked man.

Thorpe finished that whole 90 minutes, but only just. He was injured during a goalmouth scramble with 20 minutes left, but no trainer was at any time called to give him first aid. Referee Warr said later that he had asked Thorpe if he needed attention, and the young keeper had indicated he was fit enough to continue – which is not quite the same thing. It should not be forgotten that in 1936 no substitutes of any kind were allowed. There was great pressure on players, particularly goalkeepers occupying their specialist position, to limp through the whole of a match.

Neither did any of his team-mates notice anything wrong as they left the pitch – 'Jimmy appeared to be all right and made no complaint of feeling ill.' Consequently they were devastated when they reported for training four days later, on Wednesday, 5 February 1936, and were told that Thorpe had died in Monkwearmouth and Southwick Infirmary in the early hours of that morning. The report of the Coroner's Inquest was fiercely critical of the referee for not taking better control of a rough match, suggesting that the violence of the play itself triggered off the diabetic coma which led quickly to the young man's death. A separate four-man commission, appointed by the FA later that month to examine the incident, exonerated both the referee and the game of football itself. While accepting that the Chelsea match precipitated the coma which cost Thorpe his life, the FA suggested that the fact he had previously played 139 league and cup games without any apparent ill effects meant that no official or opponent could in the slightest degree be held responsible for Jimmy Thorpe's tragic death.

Football was found not guilty of the goalkeeper's murder – and it is difficult to see what other verdict could have been returned. But to Sunderland supporters then and later, Jimmy Thorpe was a martyr to the cause. For many years he would be included in lists of men and women killed by sport.

Thorpe's 1935–36 league championship medal was presented to his widow. Sunderland handed out three of the baubles to goalkeepers that spring. Matt Middleton stepped in for nine games to replace the boy who had earlier replaced him. After a traumatic 6–0 defeat at Ayresome Park, Middleton himself was shunted aside to make room for another youngster – Johnny Mapson from Reading. Mapson promptly proceeded to save three of the first four penalties taken against him and his name would still be found in the team lists of Sunderland AFC almost 20 years later!

That game at Middlesbrough became notable for yet another memorable trough in the up-and-down second half of Sunderland's championship season. It was unusual enough for the champions-elect to get beaten 6–0 by a side struggling in the relegation zone; but this Middlesbrough v. Sunderland game was possibly the most evil-tempered in a long line of derby contests which were, to speak kindly of them, rarely polite.

Sunderland, on top of the table and *en route* to the title, were expected to take both points home from Ayresome Park on 28 March 1936. They had just suffered their worst spell of the season in the league, losing two and drawing two of their previous four matches; but their points total was by then so great that the Wearsiders were still on top of Division One. And where better to end the lean period than at the home of Middlesbrough, never a serious threat to Sunderland's north-eastern dominance, and in the March of 1936 precariously placed towards the bottom of the First Division? Raich Carter had missed the previous match through injury, but he was now fit again. The team was back to full strength and the fans travelled south expecting a win. Johnny Cochrane and his players also hoped to win, but were prepared to settle for a draw. What happened next became legendary on Teesside.

In no time at all Middlesbrough went 3–0 up. Egged on by the partisan supporters of both teams, 'tempers grew hot, and incidents and fouls flowed thick and fast.' This degeneration of the footballing aspect of the match aided Middlesbrough rather than the skilful (and as Charlie Buchan pointed out, not physically robust) Sunderland players. With 15 minutes left Middlesbrough were 5–0 ahead. Most of the Sunderland squad, particularly the forward line, was at this stage just anxious to get out of there; to hear the final whistle, escape from Ayresome Park with their skins and limbs intact, and put that terrible result behind them.

The slight figure of Raich Carter was congratulating himself at having steered clear of trouble when the ball came to him. He set off downfield and beat two men, but in getting past a 'Boro half-back he pushed the ball too far. The Middlesbrough full-back Brown raced to intercept – and as Brown and Carter converged on the ball Carter attempted to hook it with outstretched leg into the middle. He missed and caught Brown's knee, and Brown went down like a sack of coal. The referee appeared instantly on the spot and, in a clear attempt to impose order on a match which had long since slipped out of his control, he sent Carter off for the first and only time in the inside-forward's career. He was never before or since so much as cautioned, let alone sent off. Carter was flabbergasted, and even the Middlesbrough captain Bobby Baxter pleaded with the referee that it had been an accidental foul – a free-kick, yes, but not even a bookable offence let alone a sending-off one. It was of course no use. The referee's finger pointed adamantly at the changing room and Carter walked.

He had no sooner got inside, and was beneath the stand explaining what had happened to reserve Sandy McNab, than their team-mate, right-winger Bert Davis, who had also just returned to the side after a period of injury, came trooping down the corridor towards them.

'He's been sent to fetch me back!' thought Carter in a wild burst of optimism. 'It's all been a terrible mistake!'

No such luck. 'I told the ref that I didn't agree that you ought to be sent off,' said Davis. 'So he's sent me off as well for arguing.'

Four other Sunderland players were booked on 'Black Saturday', and Middlesbrough finished the game 6–0 victors, which helped to steer them clear of relegation. Such was the notoriety of the contest that the FA took the unusual step of ordering an official inquiry before the suspensions were handed down. The referee, in his report, insisted that he had seen Carter's foul intention in the player's eyes before he made contact with Brown. But the inquiry team accepted the England international's explanation, at least implicitly, for Raich received only a seven-day ban. Davis got two weeks and the four others were merely warned as to their future conduct.

That hearing did not take place until the end of April, so both players were available for the game that did win the title for Sunderland over the Easter period. It was a hectic few days. On Good Friday, 10 April 1936 they began the programme by beating Birmigham 2–1 at Roker Park before 41,000 expectant – and by this stage, extremely relieved – fans. But the next day, Saturday, they were beaten 2–1 at Bolton. These two results, along with others from the Easter period, crystallised the situation. As we have seen, Sunderland were scheduled to play their return league game with Birmingham on Easter Monday, 13 April. They needed just one point to clinch the game.

On the Sunday they travelled down from Lancashire to the midlands. In order to ease the strain of three games in four days, Johnny Cochrane and trainer Andy Reid organised a relaxing afternoon of sightseeing in Stratford-upon-Avon and in the unspoilt medieval Worcestershire village of Broadway. Reid was known for his strict views on athletes' diets. In the 1930s this did not mean that he insisted upon boys from Scotland and the north-east of England limiting themselves to pasta, fish and bananas, but rather that they should eat a lot of grilled or roast meat and vegetables and – crucially – avoid cakes and puddings like the plague. This regime was applied most strenuously in the 24 hours before matches.

On the eve of Sunderland AFC's most important league match in 23 years, Andy Reid's players were booked in to eat high tea at a hotel in Broadway. They sauntered in, with full and hearty appetites, and discovered a beaming manager and pinafored waitresses behind a large table groaning with cream cakes, buns, trifle, jelly – 'everything that was wrong, according to Andy, for an athlete's diet'. Reid was horrified. But it quickly became apparent that there was no alternative. The hotel staff would have been deeply offended to be asked to shovel away the puddings and serve up steak, and the players were starving. So with immense satisfaction the lads sat down and devoured the lot. And on the following day, properly fortified with cream and sugar, they murdered Birmingham by 7–2. The league had returned to Roker Park. Even better was to come.

In the absence of Alex Hastings for that crunch game at Birmingham, Johnny Cochrane made Raich Carter captain for the first time. It was a clear breach of established club policy, which had been to select the captain largely on grounds of seniority, and almost always from the half-back line. There were a number of reasons for this breaking of protocol. With the disciplinary inquiry into his sending-off at Middlesbrough about to begin, Cochrane was making public his confidence and faith in his 23-year-old prodigy (a shaken Carter had expressed fears that the sending-off might affect his England career, although in fact it did not).

The manager was also signalling his faith in the continuing attacking policy of the club, by giving the captaincy to a man who hated defensive tactics. Carter disliked tactics of any variety, for that matter, believing always that a meal together, an evening stroll, and a natter about the forthcoming game was all the mental preparation needed by top professionals. He was also famous for suggesting that if you provided two good inside-forwards, Raich Carter would give you a winning team.

The manager was preparing for the inevitable as well: Raich Carter was likely to be the dominant player in Wearside, if not English, football for a good few years; and the sooner everybody got used to that the better. So Alex Hastings, who had a good few years left in him, found himself slowly, almost imperceptibly deprived of the Sunderland skippership while he was still captain of Scotland. The manner of this steady shift of responsibility is indicative – certainly Hastings was the man being handed the league trophy at the end of the next home game, but Carter was the man in charge when the club actually won their title in such devastating fashion on the field at Birmingham five days earlier.

Cochrane confirmed this decision before the start of the 1936–37 season. Thus Raich Carter came to be the first Sunderland skipper to do something which had escaped all previous incumbents.

'Every year was to be Sunderland's cup year . . . This had to be Sunderland's year for winning the cup . . .' the weight of expectation on the Roker players as this oldest and most desirable of trophies slipped through their hands season after season was simply enormous. Over in Newcastle during their cup-winning streak of the early 1950s, Sunderland's rival north-eastern players made no secret of where their priorities lay. When it came to a cup run, they simply neglected the league matches – 'All that concerned us was winning at Wembley,' the Newcastle players would later admit; 'we stopped playing league football after the semis.'

People were beginning to believe that in the twentieth century the double was actually impossible. The mental, as well as physical, demands on professional footballers seemed so huge as to make such an achievement a thing of the distant past (the double had last been won by Aston Villa in 1897, playing 30 league games and seven cup ties, including two replays). But Sunderland were different. They never consciously favoured one tournament over the other. The Sunderland management had previously never put out a weak league side to rest players for an imminent cup tie. But unconsciously . . . well, 'the fact that Sunderland had never won the cup was a terrible thing for the north,' admitted captain Carter. And there is no doubt that Sunderland lost the league championship in the second half of the 1936–37 campaign, when they were embarked on their most promising (and certainly most strenuous) cup run since 1913. After the traditional weak beginning, five consecutive victories in October and November had put them back in the hunt to retain the title. But after the cup run started they took just 18 points from their last 21 games and finished in eighth position – and that after significantly strengthening the squad.

However it was a rough, tough cup campaign and that alone may have been enough to affect their league form. And that wasn't the whole story; if they did ease up a bit on the league with yet another cup replay looming on the horizon; if Grimsby Town did get an easy two points once the title was lost – well, nobody cared too much at the time, and after 1 May 1937 nobody cared at all.

There were two main differences between the squad which kicked off the 1935 championship season, and the First Division team a year later. One was that Johnny Mapson was easing the club's grief over the loss of Jimmy Thorpe in the best way possible, by proving himself to be at least as good a goalkeeper. Cochrane had taken a gamble on Mapson, paying Reading £2,000 when the 18-year-old had played only two matches in the Third Division (South). The gamble paid dividends.

And in January 1937 Cochrane made a brilliant purchase. Bill Murray's distinguished full-back career was coming to an end. Cochrane looked about and signed Jimmy Gorman from Blackburn Rovers. This gave Gorman's new colleagues an unrivalled opportunity for changing-room delight. Four years earlier Gorman had been the right-back who, mesmerised by a bit of Paddy Gallacher trickery at Ewood Park, had been induced to run straight into his own goalkeeper, knock him over, and then fall to the ground himself, leaving Paddy free to amble between their prostrate bodies and slip the ball into the net. Footballers do not forget such things.

Both those men were bought in especially to do a job. The rest of the first team squad were not. A good proportion of the remainder of the side – Carter, Gurney, Duns, the young winger from Deneby Colliery, Eddie Burbanks – were north-easterners. Most of the rest were Scots. But they all had at least one thing in common: they had worked their way up through the ranks at Roker Park; they were former reserve team players, if not juniors. They were part of the family.

As ever, there was an unpromising start to the cup campaign. Sunderland were drawn in the third round away to Southampton. The previous Saturday the new captain, Raich Carter, tore a leg muscle in a 1–1 draw at Arsenal. He travelled south with the club and gave the injured leg a late test by sprinting along the tube platform at Waterloo Station, but failed himself and sat out the game. Southampton, sitting in the bottom half of Division Two, were not the most severe of tests – but then, nor had been Port Vale. Sunderland were happy enough to return home with a 3–2 win.

Then the fun really started. In the fourth round the club drew yet another middling Second Division side, Luton Town away. And once again they toyed with elimination. On 30 January 1937 the Kenilworth Road ground was frozen solid. Sunderland displayed their continuing inability to function on such surfaces and Luton went in at half-time with a 2–0 lead. Luckily it began to rain in the second half, the ground duly softened, and the reigning champions began to play. A goal from each winger, Len Duns and Jimmy Connor, was enough to salvage a 2–2 draw and a replay at Roker. 'There was not a man in the team, however, who did not feel that we were still lucky to be in the competition.' The softening ground, it was generally agreed, had saved Sunderland. 'Personally I am all in favour of watering football pitches,' Raich Carter would say, 'and would like to see the practice made compulsory. In the first place it reduces the risk of serious injury . . . In the second place good football needs a yielding pitch. A light ball on a hard ground is extremely difficult to control. It becomes almost impossible to keep the ball low and pass accurately.'

Connor and Duns scored again in the replay four days later, and one from Carter helped Sunderland gain an easy 3–1 win. But for the Scottish international Jimmy Connor it was a victory tinged with disaster. After scoring he picked up an injury which put him out for the rest of the season, and which – although Sunderland kept him on the books for a further three years – effectively ended his career. From that day onwards the young winger from Deneby Colliery, Eddie Burbanks, claimed his place.

The fifth round opposition also came from the bottom half of Division Two, and this time Sunderland displayed no nerves in getting rid of Swansea Town by 3–0 at Roker. In the sixth they faced their first top-flight opposition, the formidable Wolverhampton Wanderers who would finish second in the league that year, one point behind Arsenal. A record 57,751 crowded into Molineux (official capacity 55,000) to see Welsh international Bryn Jones give Wolves the lead, which Len Duns equalised to take the tie back to Roker Park. Wolves, it was happily noted, had amply watered their pitch beforehand.

The replay before 61,796 Wearsiders was an astonishing affair. Goalless for most of the 90 minutes, Wolves took a 1–0 lead with just four minutes left. Sunderland pressed forward frantically, and in the last minute won a throw-in on the right flank. Little Charlie Thomson quickly threw it to Raich Carter; Carter returned the ball first-time to Thomson; and the right-half promptly swung it across the edge of the box. There Bobby Gurney stuck out a hopeful right foot and made contact. It seemed that the whole of the Wolves team was packed inside their penalty area, but Gurney's soft shot miraculously bounced through the lot of them and past the keeper's grasping right hand to come to rest in the bottom corner of the net. 'I doubt,' said one reporter, 'if there has ever been such pandemonium at Roker Park.'

From then on Sunderland held the whip-hand. In extra-time Duns scored yet again to give them the lead, and although Wolves managed to equalise and force a second replay, Cochrane's tail was up. He and his players felt that they had the measure of Wolves, barring unforeseen circumstances.

And those unforeseen circumstances almost emerged. The third quarter-final against Wolverhampton Wanderers was scheduled for 15 March 1937 at Hillsborough. Shortly before the game goalkeeper Johnny Mapson received a letter 'asking me if I'd be interested in earning some money by giving Wolverhampton the chance of winning'. Mapson took the note to Cochrane 'and that was the last I heard of it'. Mapson kept a clean sheet in the third and conclusive game, while at the other end Charlie Thomson and the deadly triumvirate of Carter, Gurney and Gallacher each scored to settle the issue, after five hours of football, by 4–0.

Sunderland were in the semi-finals, and on the face of things they could not have had an easier draw. They were to play Millwall at Huddersfield, and Millwall played their league football in the Third Division (South). But the lesson of Port Vale was particularly apt. Millwall had won through six rounds of cup competition to reach these semi-finals, knocking out in the process two First Division clubs, Derby County and Manchester City. And for a while they rattled Sunderland, taking a 1–0 lead early in the game. But Bobby Gurney equalised before half-time, and in the second half Paddy Gallacher made it 2–1 from a corner. Millwall pressed hard towards the end, but when the final whistle blew Sunderland's players were able to relax with one happy common thought: 'We're at Wembley now!'

With the league effectively lost after the beginning of April, Johnny Cochrane took the step – unusual for Sunderland – of 'resting' some members of his chosen first eleven in the following weeks. Two days after the Millwall semi-final Sunderland visited Grimsby Town. Of his regular first-team squad he played just three: Mapson, Duns and Burbanks. It showed. Grimsby won 6–0, a sensational victory over the reigning league champions and FA Cup finalists which helped the Humberside team to evade relegation at the expense of Manchester City. As if to make amends, when City themselves visited Roker two days later Cochrane added only Gorman and Thomson to his depleted team. City won 3–1. They still went down. Only in the last league game of the season did Cochrane give his cup final side an outing. They lost to Leeds at Elland Road by 3–0. They may not have been fully committed.

Certainly, the players had other things on their minds. Since

Sunderland's last cup final appearance in 1913 the professional game had changed. Soccer in the 1930s had become a big-money sport. It was attracting more paying customers than ever before, or than it ever would again. Consequently it also attracted all of the seedy side of unfettered capitalism. Sunderland captain Raich Carter would remember well the weeks between the semi-final and Wembley, and for many of the wrong reasons:

> The hordes of previously unknown 'friends' ringing you up, writing you letters, calling at your private address, buttonholing you in the street – all after one thing: Cup final tickets. The 'wide' boys, the professional ticket touts, muscled in, flashing their pound notes and talking, bullying, cajoling for tickets. They call at your home when you are out. They swear to your womenfolk that you have said it's all right to hand over the tickets: you've done a deal with them.
>
> A player would not mind so much if it were only he personally who was getting pestered. But when he returns home – as I know many have done – to find his wife reduced to tears by the incessant stream of badgering callers who have refused to believe that there are no tickets in the house, then it hits him in a vulnerable spot and adds an unnecessary worry to those pre-Cup final days.

On 1 May 1937 the waiting was over. The Sunderland changing room at Wembley was a cheerful, optimistic place, bustling with directors, friends, family and even some fans. Johnny Cochrane's instructions to his players were short and sweet: 'Cover up well, and the nearest man go for the ball.'

Carter lost the toss, but it seemed not to matter. The day was bright and fine, with hardly a breath of wind. There was no obvious advantage in choosing ends. But Sunderland started badly. They failed to find any rhythm, and Preston slowly began to dominate the game. Half-way through the first half North End took a deserved lead. Their centre-forward Frank O'Donnell picked up a pass, beat centre-half Bert Johnston, and ran through to score past Mapson.

This could have had a serious psychological effect on Sunderland. Not only were the old superstitions of an FA Cup jinx aroused, but it happened to be a fact that in all of the previous Wembley finals, the team that scored first had won the cup. And Preston almost did double their lead. Fifteen minutes after going 1–0 up O'Donnell was racing through on Mapson again, with Johnston in pursuit. This time Bert pulled the centre-forward down just outside the box. It was before the days of automatic dismissals. Preston were given a free-kick, which they squandered, and Johnston was not even booked.

At half-time, over a cup of tea, somebody said O'Donnell must be 'stopped at all costs'. Carter disagreed. 'It's more important to score our own goals,' said the captain. 'We've got to be more in the game. We've got to make the ball work more, find the man more. Don't be nervous. Let's play football as we can play it and we'll be all right.'

In Johnny Mapson's words: 'In the second half there was only one team in it,' and that team was Sunderland. Shortly after the restart the Wearsiders won a corner out on the left. Eddie Burbanks swung it in; Raich Carter headed it forward and Bobby Gurney, standing with his back to goal a few feet out, back-headed the ball into the Preston net. The Lancashire team appealed vainly for offside, but full-back Andy Beattie had been playing Gurney on and the equaliser stood.

Tails up, Sunderland laid siege to the Preston goal. Carter had one golden opportunity, but mishit his shot into the side-netting, before he finally put his team ahead. A ball bounced invitingly, awkwardly, into the centre: Carter quickly darted through the inside-left channel, beat the full-back and the Preston keeper to the ball and lobbed it over the two of them just as all three players went down in a heap. The ball found the back of the net and Sunderland were 2–1 ahead. Paddy Gallacher laid on the third, slipping a beautifully weighted pass inside the North End defence for Eddie Burbanks to race through and push it home from an angle. The final whistle blew at 3–1.

They had played their first FA Cup tie on 8 November 1884. After 53 years of trying, the FA Cup was finally on its way to Sunderland. And it was some homecoming. The team had a weekend in London before returning north on the Monday in a special Pullman train decked in red and white. The crowds on passing stations grew in number as the train passed Grantham, Doncaster, York and Darlington – until each platform was packed with people waving red and white scarves and cheering. When the Pullman arrived at Newcastle the mayor and the town band appeared to give the Geordies' great rivals a civic welcome.

But all that paled beside the reception on Wearside. The train from Newcastle stopped at Monkwearmouth. There the players walked through the station yard to board open coaches which would carry them and the FA Cup on a four-mile procession through Sunderland to the Town Hall. The moment they stepped outside Monkwearmouth Station, recalled Raich Carter, who was carrying the cup, everything went off:

> The tugs and ships in the river were hooting and blowing their sirens, railway engines shrilled their whistles, bells rang and rattles clacked, there was shouting and cheering.
>
> It was like a thick concrete wall of deafening din. Then the cheering resolved itself into a Sunderland roar: 'Ha-way the lads!' And the cry was taken up and surged round, echoing and re-echoing through the crowd who spread further than the eye could see. 'Ha-way, ha-way, ha-way!' cried half a million throats.

The front coach carrying the team and cup was followed by two more with players' wives, directors and officials; led by the local Police Band, they edged their way through an incredible mass of humanity. Children clambered over bridges and walls for a better view. Flags and bunting which had recently been used for the coronation of the King and Queen who had presented the cup, were brought out once more. 'Sunderland had gone crazy.'

At the Town Hall the Mayor of Sunderland told the assembly: 'They played a good, clean game and they are clean, good-living lads who bring credit to themselves not only on the football field but in their private lives.' Roker Park had been thrown open to the public, and the procession next made its way there in the early summer's night. Supporters dressed in red and white suits and dresses danced up and down the terracing as the team paraded the trophy around the touchline – with the Police Band still faithfully leading the way – before Jimmy Cochrane, Bobby Gurney and Raich Carter placed the FA Cup on the centre spot and the national anthem was sung. Dancing and singing continued on the streets of Sunderland past midnight and throughout the early hours of Tuesday morning. Those bottles of beer which had been laid down unopened following defeat in 1913 had long been drunk. It was said that no ale ever tasted sweeter.

Having tasted cup success Sunderland could hardly wait for a second bite. The league, that sustainer of the club's fortunes throughout its formative years, seemed almost to go by the board as Cochrane's men looked forward to defending the FA Cup. By the half-way stage at the end of December 1937 Sunderland sat in mid-table. They would finish eighth. They had in the end a major second-hand influence on the destination of the title. In the last game of the season, Wolves travelled to Roker needing just a point to snatch the championship from Arsenal at the very last. Sunderland AFC took the opportunity to show the midland upstarts who was really in charge by turning on a vintage display and winning 1–0. Arsenal took the league by one point.

But at the turn of the year even that small consolation was in the future. At the beginning of 1938 it was clear that Sunderland were not going to win the league themselves – and nobody really cared. January meant that FA Cup time was here again . . .

The excitement was reflected in the gates. In the third round Sunderland were drawn at home to non-league side Watford, and almost 36,000 paid to see them sneak through with a single goal from Len Duns.

The fourth round saw another momentous clash with Everton who, two years earlier, had beaten Sunderland 6–4 in that epic tie at Goodison Park. Bobby Gurney gave the Wearsiders a first-half lead and then the tables turned. Everton spent the entire second period laying siege to Sunderland's goal. 'We just weren't in it,' recalled goalkeeper Johnny Mapson, who was widely regarded to have had the best 45 minutes in his career. 'To this day I'll never know how we kept the ball out of the net, everything just seemed to finish up in my hands. I don't think we got the ball over the half-way line more than twice in the second half . . . They were all over us.' On one occasion Everton's brilliant, record-breaking international centre-forward Tommy Lawton met the ball with his forehead as it flew across the six-yard box, and fired in what seemed a certain goal. Lawton then looked up to see Mapson holding the ball in his hands. 'Lucky bastard!' he said. Luck or brilliance, Mapson held out, and Sunderland won 1–0.

They then dismissed Second Division Bradford Park Avenue at Roker, also by 1–0, with almost 60,000 north-easterners saluting another cup goal from Duns (he had netted five in the previous year's run to the final).

Then, in the quarter-finals, came Tottenham Hotspur away. A standing ground record of 75,038 packed into White Hart Lane on 5 March 1938 – and Raich Carter noted that 'there seemed to be as many people present from the north as there were Spurs supporters. At least they made as much noise.'

A taut, thrilling contest remained goalless until well into the second half, when Eddie Burbanks broke down the left wing and pushed a short, low ball into the middle. Raich Carter, lurking dangerously, controlled it and then banged it into the back of the net. There was a second of absolute silence in White Hart Lane, before a tumultuous roar broke out from the Sunderland fans packed high at the back of the old stand – a roar which quickly segued into a stirring rendition of 'Blaydon Races'.

Cochrane made all possible preparations for his second successive FA Cup semi-final. It would be against Huddersfield Town – by common consent a reduced force since the departure of their great manager Herbert Chapman to Arsenal – at Blackburn. The squad trained intensively in mild March weather at Southport. They were supremely confident. Virtually the whole first eleven had walked away from Wembley a year earlier carrying the FA Cup and they firmly believed that after the cauldrons of Goodison and White Hart Lane the worst of the 1938 campaign was behind them. What was more, Preston North End – the previous year's beaten opponents in the final – also appeared destined for Wembley in 1938 once more. Preston were facing Second Division Aston Villa in the other semi-final on 26 March. Surely a re-run of the 1937 final was on the cards?

Preston got there, and this time they won the cup. But in doing so they beat Huddersfield Town; for Huddersfield knocked Sunderland out of the semis by 3–1. It was a dismal Sunderland performance – 'our play was certainly sluggish; we never got going at all.' For the first time in three years, Sunderland finished the season without a major trophy.

Matters did not improve. The season 1938–39 yielded results in the league which were simply the worst since Johnny Cochrane's arrival ten years earlier. By the end of December 1938 it was clear that rather than jousting for the title, Sunderland would be scuffling to avoid relegation. Then the cup came round again. A third round dismissal of Second Division Plymouth Argyle was no more than the fans expected. The fourth round, however, contained a wonderful boost with the 2–0 defeat of Middlesbrough on Teesside. Then came the fifth round, and yet another of the marathon cup duels to which Sunderland were becoming accustomed. This one would have extra significance, however. It would prove – for different reasons – to be the last great football contest that the manager and the vast majority of his players would ever enter in the colours of Sunderland AFC.

The 1939 fifth round tie was against Blackburn – fittingly, the owners of the ground upon which Huddersfield had knocked Sunderland out a year before. The first game, at Roker Park, was a 1–1 draw. The second, at Ewood Park, finished 0–0 after extra time. The third replay took place at Hillsborough on 18 February.

In the second minute Carter sent Bobby Gurney free through the middle. Gurney was challenged by the Blackburn keeper Barron; both men went down; the ball ran free to Len Duns, whose shot was headed off the line. But then the attention turned to Gurney, who was still on the turf and clearly in pain. He went off on a stretcher for treatment, but returned after a few minutes and hobbled through until half-time, when he stayed off. This was not surprising. Bobby Gurney had broken his leg. That marvellous club servant, the boy signed from Bishop Auckland back in 1925, who had played in 388 matches and scored 228 goals, and whose playing career had slowly been winding down – Bobby Gurney would never kick another ball for Sunderland.

The ten remaining men battled bravely through the rest of this fateful cup-tie. It was 0–0 after 90 minutes, and it was still 0–0 with three minutes to go of extra time. Then a header from Blackburn's centre-half Pryde beat Mapson and was dipping under the bar. Raich Carter jumped and fisted it over the bar. A penalty was awarded (and in those lenient times, Carter was not even booked) – but Pryde hit the spot-kick wide. Another replay seemed imminent, this time with 11-a-side. Sunderland relaxed – too early. In the dying seconds Blackburn won a free-kick outside the box. Left-winger Guest struck it over Mapson and into the far corner for the winner. Sunderland had lost 1–0.

They were out of the cup, they had lost their most consistent and possibly their best-loved forward, and now they would lose their manager. Two weeks later, after a 3–0 league defeat at Middlesbrough which left the club dangerously exposed in the bottom half of Division One, on 3 March 1939 Johnny Cochrane resigned.

Cochrane, the short, ebullient, vocal, disciplinarian Scot, may not have been the club's most successful manager. That honour should still be paid to Tom Watson with his three league titles. But Johnny Cochrane remains the only manager to have taken both the league championship and the FA Cup to Roker Park. In doing so, he had built a superb attacking football team; a side which refused to know the meaning of defeat or of defensive play; a squad built on a mix of local youth and (largely Scottish) experience. He would be replaced in the long term by one of those experienced Scots. The long-serving full-back Bill Murray had left for St Mirren, carrying his championship medal, in 1936. In the summer of 1939 he agreed to return to Wearside as manager. For the remainder of the 1938–39 season club secretary George Crow took care of the team, steering them safely into 16th position.

At the start of the 1939–40 season Bill Murray's squad played just three games. The third of them, away to Arsenal on 2 September 1939, attracted the extraordinarily low crowd of 5,000 people. The populations of London and the north-east had other things on their mind. The match kicked off at the unusually late hour of 5 p.m. Outside Highbury Stadium – where Ted Drake was scoring four in his team's 5–1 win over Sunderland – many of the streets were designated as one-way traffic to accommodate the flow of evacuees from the metropolis. That morning Adolf Hitler's *Wehrmacht* had invaded Poland. The next day, 3 September, Britain declared war on Germany. Organised professional soccer was once more suspended.

SEVEN

The Bank of England Team

1939–1957

To put it kindly, the post-war team enjoyed the most bizarre period in the history of Sunderland AFC. Bill Murray managed to spend extraordinary sums of money and to assemble some of the best and most famous footballers in the club's existence. They played before – on average – the biggest and most vocal crowds ever assembled on Wearside (it was in this period that the reputation of the famous 'Roker roar' was established throughout the kingdom).

But they won nothing. And at the end of their highly publicised era the good name of the football club was dragged through the mud. When it all blew up the fall-out swept away the entire management team, forcibly retired virtually all of the board and threatened to halve the playing staff. And in retrospect it was worse even than that. For this wasted period can now be seen as a vitally important part of the club's story. It led to a decline which was to take almost half a century to reverse. That decline would of course be punctuated by moments of great joy, of passion and brilliance. But as a long-term trend it was undeniable. And it began when Bill Murray surveyed his war-torn team and ravaged stadium, as professional football prepared to recommence in the first weeks of 1946.

Murray did not lose any of his playing staff through death on the battlefield. There was an explanation for this. As in the First World

War, many Sunderland players went to work in the 'protected essential industries' of the north-east, such as the collieries and the shipyards, where labour was deemed to be of equal importance to joining the armed forces. Some of course did join up, but they were thankfully spared.

Like everybody else, the players' war began on the Sunday morning following that 5–1 defeat at Highbury on 2 September 1939. They gathered around the radio at 11 a.m. in London's Russell Hotel to hear Prime Minister Chamberlain declare war on Germany. They heard the air-raid sirens go off shortly afterwards, and the whole team ran out into Russell Square to see what was happening, before being chased back inside by an Air Raid Warden. They were sent up to the third floor, where there was supposedly less danger from flying glass, and they sat on the floor until the all-clear sounded. Then they caught the train back to Sunderland, knowing that nothing would be the same again.

They wandered down to Roker Park on Monday morning. They had a midweek game scheduled at Charlton Athletic, but nobody at the club could tell the players what was happening. They drew their pay and went home. They returned on Tuesday, mooched dispiritedly around, and went away again. On Wednesday they were told that the midweek match, and Saturday's fixture at home to Blackpool, were both off. They did not even have the heart to kick a ball around. On the following Monday they were given half a week's wages (four pounds) and told that they and the club were – for the foreseeable future – finished.

Sunderland initially stayed out of the wartime north-eastern regional league, entering it only in 1941. In 1942 they reached the semi-final of the League War Cup, fielding a team with only one or two recognisable faces such as Raich Carter, who was working as a Physical Training Instructor for the RAF at a local base.

The club then resumed full participation in the wartime competitions. These were haphazard affairs, involving whoever might be in the area at the time. Aldershot Football Club, for instance, enjoyed a particularly successful period between 1939 and 1945, being able at times to field almost a full international team by drawing on conscripts from the local barracks. Sunderland were not nearly so blessed, although Hastings, Gorman and Burbanks were still occasionally available as well as Carter. An idea of the melting pot of wartime soccer can be gleaned from the fact that both Jackie Milburn and Stan Mortenson, who would become more famous in the colours of Newcastle United and Blackpool, played for Sunderland in 1943.

It was in March 1943 that the war made its deepest impression on Roker Park. Bombs fell on the pitch and just outside the ground in March 1943, killing a policeman, and two months later the car park and the clubhouse were destroyed in another raid.

When peace in Europe was declared in 1945, the FA decided to reintroduce the FA Cup early in 1946, and the Football League started again in the autumn of 1946. The team that Bill Murray put out in January for the first games of the 1946 cup competition contained Mapson, Hastings, Duns, Burbanks and half-back Arthur Housam, who had been signed from Hylton Colliery in 1937.

The one glaring absence was Horatio Carter. At the age of 31 Carter hoped that Sunderland would put him on an extended contract immediately after the war, thereby giving him the security (and possibility of further benefit matches) to see out his career on Wearside. Still an England international, and kept fit by his activities as a PTI in the RAF during the conflict, Carter had every reason to expect that his home town team would respond positively to this request from their former captain.

But Sunderland put him on the transfer list. During the war Carter's home in Sunderland had been bombed and his wife had gone to live with her family in Derby. So Derby County snapped him up. Sunderland lost the man that the veteran local reporter Arthur Appleton described as the club's 'most consistently effective inside-forward since Buchan. He had a hard left-foot drive, the finest body swerve I have ever seen, and, with it all, he was capable of an astonishingly direct dash goalwards. He positioned astutely, and was a great believer in making the ball do the work. He always retained, too the capacity he had as a schoolboy, for losing himself in a game – of being utterly absorbed in it.' He also scored 130 goals in 279 appearances for his hometown club.

Carter did not leave the most popular of reputations behind him in the north-east, for a local boy who captained Sunderland to such success, and who personally achieved such success for England (his first cap came in 1933 and his last in 1947). There were a number of reasons for his not finding the popularity that blunt statistics suggest he was due – the popularity that, for instance, his team-mate and fellow north-easterner Bobby Gurney achieved. Carter was a naturally diffident man, slow to show his undoubted emotion and commitment. His reputation was also damaged by the fact that when war broke out he joined the fire service rather than the armed forces. And the manner of his leaving on a £6,000 transfer to Derby County was interpreted by some as self-serving treachery.

He did not deserve the ill-feeling. The fact that Raich Carter left Sunderland at all was the fault of the club's manager and directors, who would not have had to work too hard (or to spend too much) to keep him. Carter himself was right to suggest that he could have expected better, after all he had done for the club.

Sunderland were certainly given reason to lament his passing. The first FA Cup of the post-war years was played on a home-and-away basis, each tie taking place over two legs. Sunderland went out in the fifth round, losing 3–2 on aggregate to Birmingham City. Birmingham went on to the semi-finals, where they were dismissed by Derby County, thanks to the goals of their new inside-right, Horatio Carter. Derby had been in the Football League for two years longer than Sunderland, and had never won the FA Cup. Carter was accustomed to putting such little things right. His new club Derby, beat Charlton Athletic in the 1946 cup final by 4–1.

Two years after Carter's departure Sunderland bought the footballer they hoped would replace him. He was an outspoken 26-year-old Yorkshireman who had already been picked for

England at inside-left, and who was known to be dissatisfied with his current club, Newcastle United. Billy Murray swooped and paid £20,050 for Len Shackleton. Nobody knew it at the time, but that fee marked the beginning of the 'Bank of England team'.

'The Clown Prince of Soccer', as Shackleton would christen himself, certainly provided entertainment. But his début was horribly ominous. It was a league game on 14 February 1948, away to Derby County. Shackleton had created national headlines by his First Division début for Newcastle 16 months earlier, scoring six goals in a 13–0 thrashing of Newport County. Could he do the same for Sunderland against Derby? Probably not, but Sunderland's keeper Johnny Mapson told his colleagues – and the new signing – not to worry about the opposition's number eight, Raich Carter. 'Just let him shoot,' said Mapson. Carter did shoot, and scored four in a 5–1 Derby win. Shackleton failed to find the net.

Sunderland had to rebuild. The handful of experienced players left in 1946 and 1947 from the 1939 team were not getting any younger. The wartime fixtures had brought in some local boys like Tommy Reynolds from Felling, Bill Walsh from Horden, and – most rewardingly – the full-back Jack Stelling of Washington, who was signed from Usworth High Grange and who would dominate his position for the best part of nine seasons.

But it was widely accepted that these were not enough – certainly not enough to replace such champions and cup-winners as Carter, Gurney, Gallacher and company. So Sunderland dipped into their ample coffers and bought.

At first they contented themselves with a mission to bring back local boys from far afield. The Northumbrian English international inside-right Jackie Robinson was picked up from Sheffield Wednesday early in the 1946–47 season. The centre-forward Ron Turnbull from Blyth was bought from Dundee – and unlike Len Shackleton, Turnbull was to enjoy an outstanding first match, scoring all Sunderland's goals in a 4–1 defeat of Portsmouth on 29 November 1947.

But these were clearly not enough. In the January of 1948

Sunderland lost four consecutive league games, dropped towards the bottom of the league, and were knocked out of the third round of the FA Cup by Second Division Southampton. That was followed by a 1–0 home league defeat at the hands of Manchester City, which sent the club even closer to the danger zone. The directors responded by going into closed session for an hour immediately after the Manchester City game. They decided at that meeting to bid £12,000 for a player from the Third Division (North). He was Carlisle United's brilliant inside-right and player-manager, Ivor Broadis. Broadis had made it clear that he was willing to leave Carlisle, but he was still under contract, and the deal was off – for the moment.

So they paid £20,000 for Len Shackleton instead. It did not pay off. A string of persistently poor results saw the club hovering about the relegation area for all of the second half of the season – and in the end they were saved only by the inferior form of the two beneath them, the relegated Blackburn and Grimsby. The support, however, was still sensational. Even battles against the drop drew them to Roker. When Blackpool visited for the crucial second-last home game of the season – a game which Sunderland had to win to lift themselves clear of the bottom two – a league ground record of 61,084 (it would stand for just two years) turned up to see a single goal from pre-war signing Dick Davis ensure the two vital points.

So Sunderland survived the Division One season of 1947–48 in 20th place in a 22-team First Division. But holding their record of being the only top flight side never to have been relegated was not quite enough. Nonetheless, Billy Murray persevered with the squad he had assembled until an even worse catastrophe.

The 1948–49 league season was marginally better than its predecessor. The club never looked like challenging for the title, but a comfortable mid-table place was better than the bottom four, and everybody could tell themselves that the light was visible at the end of the tunnel. Disaster struck – as always – in the FA Cup. Sunderland got through to the fourth round by dismissing Third

Division Crewe Alexandra by 2–0. Then they drew the perennial giant-killers, non-league Yeovil Town.

Yeovil's reputation was not then what it would become (what it would become, it should be said, with no small help from their result against Sunderland AFC). But the writing was on the wall. Yeovil had defeated Second Division Bury by 3–1 in the third round and the celebrated part-timers had, as player-manager, a particularly brilliant inside-forward with a terrific future in the professional game named Alec Stock. They also had a famous, formidable sloping pitch, and a fanatical 13,500 west country support who believed, like their players, that Yeovil Town was capable of beating the best in the land.

In retrospect, it is easy to see the First Division thoroughbreds from Wearside arriving in this unfamiliar cauldron as lambs to the slaughter. The whole country was so prepared for an upset that, when it came, this most famous of cup 'shocks' was almost expected. In the days before *Match Of The Day* the Gaumont British News film cameras were in attendance; and Raymond Glendinning was present, commentating live on BBC Radio.

The packed crowd, tiny by Roker standards, was nonetheless formidable. The west country yokelry sat on stacked beer crates instead of terracing, a public holiday was declared in Yeovil, shops were painted in the club's colours of green and white – it was, remembered Alec Stock, 'a real gala atmosphere'. Stock would also claim that 'the opposition were already frightened of our reputation'. Sunderland may not have been all that intimidated, but they certainly found the experience unusual. 'I remember running out,' said full-back Jack Stelling, 'and there were people sitting on the touch-line. We weren't used to this sort of thing.'

Alec Stock put Yeovil ahead, but Jackie Robinson equalised following a mistake by Dickie Dyke, the Yeovil reserve keeper (a solicitor's clerk). It stayed 1–1 until the 90-minute final whistle. Ordinarily, that would have been that. Yeovil would have travelled to Roker for the replay in the following week, and been comprehensively dismantled. But there was a post-war production drive on in 1949, which supposedly meant that the workers had less time to watch football – and so it had been decreed that FA Cup ties should be settled whenever possible in one match, by playing extra time. So the game went into another 30 minutes. And just as the two teams turned around, fog descended. Realising that they would have little chance in a replay, Yeovil pushed fiercely forward. In the 114th minute pandemonium broke out in that tiny ground. Yeovil's Bryant scored the goal that rocked English soccer. As reporters surged across the road to telephone in their sensational copy from a local butcher's shop, Sunderland battled desperately for a replay. In the last minute they got a free-kick just outside the box. Left-back Barney Ramsden stepped up to take it – but as the crowd held its breath he stubbed his toe, and Yeovil's grateful defence booted the ball into the neighbouring allotments. Sunderland were out of the cup by 2–1, to a side not even in the Football League. 'Beating Sunderland stuck with me forever,' said Alec Stock. Although his team went out of the cup in the next round, 8–0 to Manchester United before 81,500 people at Maine Road (Old Trafford being still bomb-damaged), Yeovil would think of that day as their club's finest hour.

That strange, fog-bound cup upset in Somerset had an equally dramatic effect on the beaten side. It began the roll of the Bank of England club. The directors went into conference once more, came out of it, and promptly embarked on the biggest spending spree in Sunderland's – if not English football's – history. On the following Monday they bid, this time successfully, for Ivor Broadis. In March they landed the right-winger Tommy Wright from Partick Thistle.

At first it worked. They began scoring goals again. In 1949–50 ever-increasing crowds flocked to Roker Park to see the club become the top-scoring side in Division One. Results such as a 6–0 cup thrashing of Huddersfield, followed immediately by a 6–1 hammering of Derby County in the league, before gates of 55,000 and 62,000, put Sunderland back on the track to national dominance. A standing club record home league gate crammed through the turnstiles on 4 March 1950 when 68,004 paid to watch the 2–2 draw with Newcastle United. The big attendances for league matches were especially significant – and welcome. Before the war Sunderland had regularly drawn 50,000-plus home gates for cup games; but even in a championship season they could find themselves performing before just 15,000 or 20,000 in the league. In the 1940s and 1950s the most ordinary league season drew attendances of between 40,000 and 50,000.

The first unlikely hero of this enormous support was centre-forward Dick Davis (five goals in the two games against Huddersfield and Derby alone), who had been collected cheaply from Birmingham in the May before the Second World War, and who only slowly worked his way into Bill Murray's scheme of things.

Davis would finish that season as Division One's top scorer with 25 league goals. But Sunderland managed only third place. They lost the title in one particular traumatic – and wholly unexpected – result. On 15 April 1950 Manchester City visited the north-east. City were bottom of the table and clearly doomed to relegation. Sunderland were level-pegging at the top, and in with a great chance of the title. City had not won an away game all season. But they won this one by 2–1. Had Sunderland reversed the score-line, the fact that they lost two other (away) fixtures in the same month would not have mattered – they would have won the First Division.

The answer, decided Bill Murray and his board, was clearly to keep on buying. There was a new chairman of the directors. To great local mourning, that superb old character Colonel Joe Prior passed away in 1949. He was succeeded by a man who remembered as a boy sneaking through the railings to gain entrance to the old Newcastle Road ground – the local furniture manufacturer E.W. 'Ted' Ditchburn. To such a man, no money was too much to spend on regaining lost glory. The Bank of England team – which was actually begun under Joe Prior – took off in the hands of Ted Ditchburn.

Poor Dick Davis was the first to suffer. The league's top scorer soon found his place usurped by one of the biggest purchases of the period. His 25-goal tally was deemed to be insufficient, in view of the penetrating support provided by the likes of Shackleton and Broadis. Just a month into the 1950–51 season Aston Villa put their dynamic centre-forward Trevor Ford on the market. Chelsea, Sunderland, Cardiff and Swansea all entered the bidding for the signature of the prolific Welsh international. Murray and Ditchburn won Ford by breaking the British transfer fee record. They spent £30,000. Davis was shifted – temporarily – to inside-forward. Ivor Broadis was sold to Manchester City for £20,000.

The Ford transfer epitomised both sides of the style of the period. The arrival of this terrific footballer 'thrilled the Sunderland district' in the words of one onlooker. 'Supporters of Sunderland,' judged another expensive purchase, Len Shackleton, 'from Seaham to Shields, from Whitburn to Washington, would never recommend the scrapping of the star system: it means quite a lot to them to know that many of the big names of soccer play for the local club every Saturday.'

Those in favour of Trevor Ford and the pursuance of a big money policy very quickly got a boost: in his first home game, against Sheffield Wednesday on 4 November 1950, Ford scored three in a 5–1 win, and actually hit a shot that knocked one of the goalposts at the Fulwell end clean out of the ground!

There was certainly nothing new about a Sunderland side comprised almost entirely of imported players – the club had effectively been founded on immigrant Scots. But the north-east of England was increasingly being seen as a 'golden nursery' of talented footballers, most of whom seemed to escape the attention of the region's two big clubs. Was it not, asked some, that the easy availability of huge sums of money – handed over by enormous crowds every other Saturday – was making the Sunderland management lazy? Did not the directors prefer to buy, rather than scout and train?

And local suspicions of the 'star system' were not eased by the row that broke out after the Trevor Ford transfer. Ford made it clear that he joined Sunderland rather than his other suitors because of the Wearside club's offer of a house and a well-paid job outside football. The FA decided that he asked for rather more than that; more than the ten pound signing-on fee to which he was legally entitled. An inquiry found that he had transgressed, and fined him £100. Even then, the bold Trevor claimed to have come out on top – he had sold his story to a London newspaper for £100, and an anonymous Welsh football fan had sent him another £100 to cover the fine.

In the end his Sunderland career was not covered in glory. Len Shackleton said that 'the fining incident was the only real highlight of Fordy's career at Roker Park'. That was not quite fair. Ford played 117 cup and league games for Sunderland between 1950 and 1954, and scored the excellent total of 70 goals. But in his four seasons Sunderland finished 12th, 12th, 9th and 18th in Division One, and only once enjoyed a cup run as far as the sixth round. At least the club was able to recoup its investment – the directors got £29,500 for Trevor Ford from Aston Villa.

This underachievement reflected just as much on Len Shackleton as on Trevor Ford, of course – and on all of the other big money signings. These just kept coming in. Billy Bingham, a little right-winger who would later become famous as manager of Northern Ireland, was bought from Glentoran for £9,000 two months into the 1950–51 season. As Scottish international Tommy Wright was already capably occupying that position, the club now had two internationals competing for the number 7 shirt. It is possible, however, that manager Billy Murray possessed Scottish second sight. On 31 March 1951 Tommy Wright crashed into a post at the Roker end during a 2–0 defeat by Arsenal. It was feared that his career might be finished. Bingham consequently was allowed a free run at the right-wing slot for just over a year. Fortunately Wright recovered, and scored in his comeback game against Middlesbrough on 19 April 1952.

The solution to all these player insecurities was clearly to buy, and buy again. In November 1951 the club paid £20,000 to Third

Lanark for the Scottish international half-back George Aitken – 'a strong, hard-working player, difficult to pass'. And things did improve.

The directors' ambition was not only limited to the field of play. In the winter of 1952 the club installed floodlights at Roker Park and on 11 December Dundee arrived to christen them with a friendly. There followed an occasional night-time taste of continental opposition. Racing Club of Paris visited Wearside the following March, and – more significantly, as we shall see – Moscow Dynamo in 1955.

The club had a wonderful start to the 1952–53 season. When the third round of the FA Cup took place in January, Sunderland were on top of Division One. Goals from Bingham, Ford and Shackleton had just helped beat Arsenal 3–1 in the league.

Then Scunthorpe United of the Third Division (North) arrived at Roker Park for the cup tie on 10 January 1953. It is likely that Sunderland's fragility was not helped by a collective memory of the club's appalling record against lesser sides. Both teams scored once (Ford for Sunderland) in the dying minutes of the game on a dismal, fog-bound north-eastern afternoon. Sunderland travelled the following Wednesday to replay in Scunthorpe. It was an exceptionally close-run thing, but Ford snatched a winner – despite having unknowingly broken his ankle earlier in the game (he was out for two months). That 2–1 win should have opened the door to better things. In fact it signalled a terrible decline. Sunderland were easily dismissed from the next round of the cup, 2–0 at Burnley.

And they proceeded to draw six, lose six, and win not a single one of their next 12 league fixtures. In the late winter and spring of 1953 the Bank of England team fell from the top of Division One, to ninth in the league, where they finished. 'Those two [Scunthorpe cup] games,' that valuable witness Arthur Appleton would recall, 'seemed to affect Sunderland's confidence and, in a shaken side, personal differences came more to the fore. The Scunthorpe cup games presaged the decline that led to relegation five years later. After them, Sunderland never regained for long their old sureness.'

In the close season of 1953 relegation was a long way off, however – and anybody would have laughed at the possibility. So rich a club could not possibly be allowed to decline! So in the June of 1953 the board splashed out in the spree which got all Britain accusing Sunderland of 'attempting to buy the honours of the game with a cheque-book'. Between 11 and 23 June 1953 Sunderland spent an unprecedented £62,000 on three players. First, the Scottish team goalkeeper Jimmy Cowan was bought from Morton for £8,000. Then Arsenal were paid £27,000 for the Welsh international centre-half Ray Daniel. And a few days later the England left-winger Billy Elliott was taken off Burnley's books for £26,000.

In December that same year the inside-left Ken Chisholm was bought from Cardiff City for £15,000. And one month later, in the January of 1954, Birmingham City's Ted Purdon was bought for another £15,000 to fill the centre-forward slot vacated by the departing Trevor Ford. When the South African Ted Purdon first arrived in the Roker Park changing rooms, he – a £15,000 new boy – wandered over to say hello to the £20,000-plus players Shackleton, Daniel, and Elliott. 'You musn't mix with us,' laughed Shackleton. 'Go and talk to the other serfs and peasants!'

What with a couple of other lesser purchases, Sunderland finished that season of 1953–54 having spent about £110,000 on players – and with only one first-team regular who was not a big-money signing, right-half Stan Anderson, who had been lifted from East Durham Schoolboys in 1951. (Anderson had in fact spent his childhood kicking a makeshift ball around the back streets of Horden. He would, over the next decade, not only set an appearance record, but also experience the extreme highs and lows of the game with his local side.)

Yet they were knocked out of the third round of the FA Cup at home, 2–0, by Second Division Doncaster Rovers. And they finished fifth from the bottom of Division One, just three places clear of relegation, having conceded 89 goals in 42 matches.

What happened? 'You can't buy success,' laughed the critics. The ever-candid Len Shackleton half-agreed with them. 'There is no doubt my club made some regrettable signings,' he would write while still on Sunderland's books, 'through not making a thorough investigation of the material for which they were prepared to pay such fabulous amounts.' Twenty thousand pounds – Shackleton's transfer fee in 1948 – would be the equivalent in the year 2000 of about £325,000. Len continued:

> Directors rightly denied that team spirit was affected [by the sudden eruption of so many big-money buys into the Roker arena], but in the dressing room we knew well enough that the wheat would have to be sorted from the chaff before Sunderland started winning matches. In addition, we were not a team in the true sense of the word. When eleven famous footballers, each an individual star in his own right, are suddenly thrown together and expected to fit in as a machine, there is bound to be some discord. It takes time to harness and control a team of thoroughbreds.

Shackleton was at pains to insist that 'team spirit did not suffer', and that opinion was borne out by the one local boy in the squad of imported, expensive 'thoroughbreds'. 'There wasn't one of the big names with whom I didn't get on,' said right-half Stan Anderson later. He went on, 'They were a cheerful, happy-go-lucky bunch. And although there were some minor differences they maintained a wonderful spirit and atmosphere at Roker.'

Some others, such as the local journalist John Gibson, maintained that the great cash-splashing experiment was worth it:

> Sunderland were being built into a team that was to be renowned throughout the land as the entertainers, the great crowd-pullers. The 'Bank of England team' of the early '50s never won a major honour but they were always close –

sometimes very close. It took an open cheque-book to bring together some of soccer's greatest characters, and at the end of the era when there was nothing on the Roker mantlepiece to show for it the cynics smirked. But there is no doubt that Sunderland owed their fame to these men.

It does not take a cynic to spot the holes in that argument – even if one ignores the disgrace and ignominy which accompanied the crash of this chapter of Sunderland's history *off* the field, when the lid was at least partly lifted off the dealings which characterised the period.

There is no doubt that the Bank of England team was entertaining. 'I give our manager Billy Murray credit for usually insisting on buying ball-artists,' said Len Shackleton – and it is undeniable that a forward line containing himself, Bingham, Tommy Wright, Ford, Purdon and Chisholm was at times a breathtaking sight. But whether 'the buying spree was responsible' for Sunderland attracting some of the biggest average gates in football, as both Shackleton and Gibson suggest, is dubious. Those enormous crowds had begun to stream into Roker Park immediately after the end of the Second World War, long before the expensive players began to arrive. Then as now, football was simply hugely popular on Wearside, especially in an era when men wished to celebrate the peace by enjoying themselves – and the region did not boast too many alternative attractions. The paying public undoubtedly preferred to watch an entertaining team. But they would have also enjoyed watching a side which won the occasional trophy.

And the truth is that this team of 'thoroughbreds', far from being 'always close' to great success, were just as often uncomfortably close to disaster and humiliation. Shackleton was closer to the truth when he suggested that all of the squad had been thrown together without enough regard for the cohesion of the team; that several of them found it difficult or impossible to settle; and that some of them were just not worth the transfer fee. It is surely significant that the one sole long-term survivor of the Bank of England team was Stan Anderson – the only player who had not cost the club a penny, and the only local boy.

Goalkeeper Jimmy Cowan was the most obvious – and on the pitch, the most costly – example of the complete waste of a transfer fee. Cowan lasted just 28 games, conceded several fives, a handful of fours and one six, before being replaced by Willie Fraser, who was hurriedly bought from Airdrie for £5,000. Cowan never played another first-team match for Sunderland, and was gifted back to Third Lanark in 1955. Ironically, Fraser almost immediately replaced Cowan as the Scottish international keeper.

Neither goalkeeper was helped by the fact that the big, cheerful Welsh centre-half Ray 'Bebe' Daniel had a nightmare of a first season. Daniel was a great example of manager Murray's preference for 'scientific', thoughtful, ball-playing footballers. But in this new team, struggling to find its rhythm and some unity, and fighting one demoralising result after another, a more ordinary, steely-minded, motivating hard-man of a stopper would have been far more welcome. In the second half of the season Bebe Daniel, Sunderland's most expensive player since Trevor Ford, was relegated to the reserves. 'Remember that brief bad spell you had, Bebe?' Len Shackleton would later remind Daniel. 'From August to April?'

Ken Chisholm was somewhere in between, an undefinable half-success, half-failure. A big, strong, direct player with a quick wit and a fine line in verbal banter, Chisholm enjoyed one good season – his only full season in the first team. Half-way through his third year at Roker, this £15,000 forward was given on a free transfer to Workington Town of the Third Division (North). Along with the unhappy Cowan, Ken Chisholm could not be judged by history to have been a notably successful use of the supporters' gate-money.

The season of 1954–55 was Chisholm's one good year. In fact it saw a marked improvement in the whole squad – it was the only good year the Bank of England team really had. It would prove to be temporary, but it was the closest that Bill Murray's team came to glory in league and cup.

The biggest change happened where it was most needed – in defence. The Australian-born Scot Willie Fraser settled in comfortably behind full-backs Joe MacDonald and Jack Hedley. Hedley's had been a remarkable story. He was one of the six British football rebels (Newcastle United's future manager Charlie Mitten, and England's current centre-half Neil Franklin were among the others) who, in the post-war years, had left Europe to go to Colombia and play there. For as much as ten times a British footballer's maximum wage, they turned out for the aptly named Millonarios club of Bogotá. The Colombian league was at that time unaffiliated to FIFA, so the foreign players were promptly banned from home competition, and labelled soccer outlaws. The ban was lifted, however, in time for Hedley to resume his career at Everton, from where he moved to Sunderland in 1950.

Not until 1954 did Jack Hedley get a full season in the right-back slot, however. But he used it well. It helped that Bebe Daniel finally found his form at centre-half, in between Stan Anderson and George Aitken.

While the defence kept out the goals the forward line was netting fewer. There was no convincing out-and-out striker among them. Bingham, Shackleton, Purdon and Chisholm each managed only a modest tally, while out on the left wing the England international forward Billy Elliott, the most expensive attacker in the side, managed the extraordinary feat of playing 40 league games without scoring a single goal. Billy Murray tried to remedy this problem half-way through the season by giving East Fife £7,000 and Tommy Wright (who had drifted into the reserves) in exchange for their Scottish international inside-forward Charlie Fleming. Fleming, who was occasionally fielded in the unfamiliar centre-forward's shirt, managed half a dozen goals. It was not enough.

The result was a large number of draws – 18 in all – which cost Sunderland a real chance of the title. At the end of the 1954–55 season they finished fourth. But compensation seemed possible in that elusive temptress, the FA Cup. For a few weeks in 1955 the north-east's dream cup final, a Tyne–Wear clash between Newcastle and Sunderland, looked to be on the cards. Sunderland would certainly have relished the opportunity, smarting as the club was from Newcastle's two cup successes earlier in the decade. Excitement mounted as Preston and Swansea were both dismissed in replays, and then two Purdon goals defeated Wolves in the quarter-final at Roker Park.

When the semi-final draw was made it kept Sunderland and Newcastle apart. United had the apparently straightforward job of beating Third Division York City at Hillsborough, while Sunderland faced Manchester City at Villa Park on 26 March 1955.

The semi-final should never have taken place. Torrential storms had swept the midlands, Birmingham was flooded, and the Villa Park ground was a morass. But almost 60,000 fans from Wearside and Manchester had travelled, and it was deemed better to play than to disappoint them. So it kicked off, and in 'the mud and the pools' Charlie Fleming almost gave Sunderland what could have been a decisive lead, given the conditions and the two well-matched teams. But almost was not enough and it was City who snatched the only goal of the tie to progress, by 1–0, to the final.

Sunderland supporters' disappointment was eased slightly by the news from Hillsborough: Newcastle had been held to a draw by lowly York. This was inevitably followed by pain. The Newcastle–York replay took place, of all places, at Roker Park in the following week and Newcastle won it 2–0. In the final they beat Manchester City by 3–1.

It had been, in the end, an anti-climactic season. But the semi-final of the FA Cup and fourth place in the league was infinitely better than being knocked out of the third round by some bunch of hackers from the lower divisions, and scrambling to avoid relegation. Here was surely hope that Ted Ditchburn's and Bill Murray's big-spending policy was finally on its way to concrete success.

The following year seemed at first to confirm this. Sunderland started brilliantly, with three league hammerings of Villa (twice, by

5–1 and 4–1) and Huddersfield (by 4–1). By November they were on top of the league. But oddly, inexplicably, once again this fickle team fell apart. And once again, the fall from grace appeared to hinge on one particular match.

In the November of 1955 Moscow Dynamo were touring Britain. The Russians were an immensely popular set of visitors – their trip around the UK immediately after the end of the Second World War was the stuff of soccer legend. So when Sunderland were selected to bring them to the north-east at the end of 1955, Roker Park was made all-ticket for this floodlit contest. The Monday night game itself was a let-down. Sunderland had fought out a torrid 4–4 draw with Burnley two days earlier, and Dynamo were by no means as strong or exciting as their team of ten years earlier. The Russians grabbed a late winner. But Sunderland had looked strangely incohesive and unconvincing. A rot seemed to set in. Ted Ditchburn and his colleagues cancelled a return invitation to Moscow. By then they had problems enough at home.

On the Saturday after the Moscow Dynamo game Sunderland, the Division One leaders, crashed to an 8–2 defeat at Luton Town. A string of mediocre results took the club up to Boxing Day, having slipped from the top. There followed an extraordinary 48 hours. On 26 December 1955 Newcastle United were due at Roker in the league. On 27 December Sunderland were scheduled to return the favour by visiting St James's Park.

Newcastle won the Roker game by 6–1. Murray and Ditchburn acted with extraordinary speed, going and signing the Burnley centre-forward Bill Holden *that same night*. Holden was consequently available for selection the next day at Newcastle. He was picked. He even scored. But Newcastle won 3–1. Holden played a further 23 league and cup games that season, scoring a total of seven goals. In October 1956 – ten months after his whirlwind signing – he was transferred to Stockport County of the Third Division (North).

This was crisis management; it was buying out of a fix; it looked what it was: panicked, ill-considered, and directionless.

But amazingly, as Sunderland went into league freefall (they took only 22 points from their last 27 games, conceding 66 goals in that period, 95 goals over the whole of the season, and with the worst defensive record in Division One they finished ninth in the table) the Bank of England team found the energy for a last cup run.

Of course this Indian summer of a doomed experiment produced some memorable, exhilarating moments. In the fifth round Sheffield United were brought back to Roker Park for a replay, and an astonishing 40-yarder from Bebe Daniel put them out 1–0. In the quarter-final Sunderland visited Newcastle United. With perfect irony, Bill Holden the player whose purchase had been prompted by that severe defeat by Newcastle two months earlier – who had in fact been bought with the single purpose of getting a result at St James's in the league – scored twice against Newcastle in the cup to put the holders out and deliver Sunderland through to their second successive semi-final.

There they lost 3–0 to Birmingham City. And the rot really set in. Charlie Fleming must at times have wondered what he was doing. Having scored 32 league and cup games in 46 matches in 1955–56, and finished up with nothing, he proceeded in 1956–57 to be just about the only Sunderland forward capable of finding the net as the club went straight to the bottom of Division One. The years of the big spend policy were almost – not quite, but almost – at an end, and there were few changes of personnel as this dreadful season began. A new young goalkeeper, the Teessider Johnny Bollands, who had been bought from Oldham earlier in the year, was promoted from the reserves after the first game of the 1956–57 season. This was because Willie Fraser found himself picking the ball out of the net six times as Sunderland once more crashed to defeat at Luton. A Scottish winger, Johnny Hannigan, was tried out wide on both the left and the right flanks for about half of the season.

And as Sunderland floundered in the relegation zone, Murray and Ditchburn made their last major withdrawal from the Bank of

England reserves. In November they spent £20,000 on the king-pin of Manchester City's so-called 'Revie plan'. Don Revie had played for City as a kind of deep-lying centre-forward, sitting behind the four other forwards and either prompting them or picking up their leavings. Sunderland used the future Leeds and England manager – when his fitness allowed – as an inside-forward.

Some change was needed. Between 22 September and 1 December 1956 Bill Murray's team played 11 league games, drew two of them, and lost the other nine. By February relegation looked more likely than not. But somehow the tired and dispirited players dredged up a last run of form in their last six league games, winning three of them and drawing the other three, to finish third from bottom, and avoid the drop. That final fling was all the more remarkable because of what was happening off the park in the early months of 1957.

Towards the end of 1956 the Football League received an anonymous letter, signed simply 'Smith'. This letter made allegations of financial irregularities at Sunderland. It suggested that undeclared payments had been made both to players and to commercial contractors. 'Smith' made his or her allegations in such depth and detail that in January 1957 – while Sunderland's expensive team was battling at the foot of Division One and being knocked out of the fourth round of the FA Cup – the League's management committee asked to see the club's books.

On 7 March 1957 a six-man commission formed jointly by the Football League and the Football Association (headed by FA chairman Arthur Drewry and League president Arthur Oakley) interviewed in Sheffield the Sunderland chairman Ted Ditchburn, director W.S. Martin, manager Bill Murray and secretary George Crow. Three weeks later, on 29 March, the commission summoned the entire Sunderland board, as well as Murray and Crow, and a solicitor representing one of the contractors, to York for a second hearing. On 10 April – just as the team on the pitch was beginning to squeeze clear of relegation – the commission published its findings. They were sensational. They created national newspaper headlines.

Basically the inquiry found that Sunderland AFC had made enormous illicit payments to its footballers – sums totalling £5,427 14s 2d. They had covered this money up by secretly paying contractors excessive amounts over five years. The contractors, who were in on the deal, had then quietly refunded the overpayment to the club in bundles of one pound notes. These one pound notes, all 5,427 of them, had then been handed out to players. Ted Ditchburn and W.S. Martin were suspended permanently from any involvement in professional football. Two other directors, Stanley Ritson and L.W. Evans, were suspended *sine die*. All the rest of the board were severely censured. And the club itself was lumbered with a fine of £5,000 the biggest ever imposed in British football, and ordered to pay the full costs of the inquiry.

That was not the end. On 16 April – three days after the end of the season – the Football Association named the guilty players. Four of them were still with the club. They were Ray 'Bebe' Daniel, Billy Elliott, Willie Fraser and Johnny Hannigan. Two others, Ken Chisholm and Trevor Ford, had left – to Workington and Holland respectively. They represented a fair selection of the Bank of England club, from first to last. All six players were summoned to the Football Association to answer allegations that they had received illegal payments. Ford, being in Holland, failed to turn up. The other five appeared, but under advice refused to answer any questions.

On 25 April all five of them were suspended *sine die* by the FA. Three weeks later, on 17 May 1957, at yet another meeting in Sheffield, the five players still in England admitted to taking underhand cash, and their suspensions were lifted. But Chisholm, Daniel and Elliott were made to forfeit two years' qualification for benefits (estimated at amounting to about £300, or £3,250 in 2000), while Fraser and Hannigan lost six months. Manager Bill Murray was also fined £200. On 26 June 1957 Murray handed in his resignation to new chairman Colonel John Turnbull. He was closely followed out of the door by trainer Bert Johnston. Murray had told the FA commission that he had handed Trevor Ford a brown paper parcel containing £250 in cash. Ford denied it, but the FA believed Murray, and the striker was banned from English football for three seasons.

Perhaps surprisingly, Sunderland received a good deal of sympathy and support during this catastrophic episode. It was widely believed that the maximum wage system was out of date – it would in fact be abolished five years later – and that such 'illegal' payments were not only commonplace but justified. The Players' Union set about collecting the names of a thousand professionals who admitted to receiving such money. Its secretary Cliff Lloyd said: 'I believe that with so many signatures before them the FA and the Football League would have no option but to declare a general amnesty.' And as if to stoke the fire, Ken Chisholm declared from Workington that Sunderland had slipped him £750 in cash when he transferred from Cardiff in 1953. Chisholm wrote to the Football League saying that he had received similar underhand payments from other clubs.

Other clubs certainly were – and continued to be – involved in the grey market of football. Most players and many officials believed that the system was so restrictive, if not endemically corrupt, as to encourage such behaviour – to make it almost excusable. But the fact remained that it was only Sunderland AFC who suffered. It was only Sunderland whose players, past and present, were penalised *en masse*. Ten others later forfeited six months' benefit qualifications for taking illegal bonuses for cup matches. It was only Sunderland who lost their chairman, their manager, and their trainer. The Bank of England club came crashing to the ground. It just was not Sunderland's summer – as if to emphasise the fact, one of the club's few players untouched by scandal, Stan Anderson, was sent off in Bulgaria in May while playing for England.

But still, at the end of July 1957, when Sunderland's shattered board appointed a new manager and coach, nobody could expect that worse was to come – or anticipate how much worse it would get. The new manager was a respected local man. Alan Brown had been born at Consett and brought up in Corbridge. As a boy he had supported Sunderland, but played as centre-half for Huddersfield, Burnley and Notts County. Brown had been trainer of Sheffield Wednesday and since 1954 manager of Burnley – establishing the unfashionable Lancashire club as a useful top-half side of Division One. Most crucially, while at Burnley he had developed a managerial philosophy which was completely contrary to the ethos of the Bank of England club. Burnley had a small support and not much money, so Alan Brown put in place a youth development system which would – even after his departure – put Burnley on an even keel at the top of the league for a good two decades.

Brown would soon be joined by a new coach, George Curtis. Curtis also had excellent qualifications. Neither of the two men, nor the directors who employed them, nor the fans who looked forward to better things, can have expected what was to happen next.

EIGHT

Brown to Brown

1957–1973

'Alan Brown,' wrote the local journalist John Gibson in a study of north-eastern footballers, 'is the most difficult and complex character I have had to write about.'

As a manager he was certainly enigmatic. Before 1958 Sunderland had never been relegated from Division One. Between 1958 and 1973 they were relegated twice – and on both occasions, Brown was manager. His saving grace, of course, was that Alan Brown was also in charge of the first Sunderland team to be promoted from Division Two.

But in 1957–58 that was in the future. Alan Brown's first season was a disaster. Early on, the club lost Len Shackleton. The ageing genius had created a bit of backroom bother during the close season by refusing to sign the Players' Union 'confession' of senior players to taking underhand money (surely, it was reasoned, if anyone took such cash it was Shack). Then, after the first match of the season, a home defeat to Arsenal in front of 56,000 faithful supporters, Shackleton felt an old injury flare up. He took medical advice and retired the following May, without having played another game after the Arsenal fixture. The Clown Prince of Soccer had set a new post-war appearance record for Sunderland with 348 games, scoring 101 goals. The fans thought he would be irreplaceable. They were right.

Sunderland went from bad to worse. By October they sat at the bottom of Division One, having just been beaten 7–0 at Blackpool and 6–0 at Alan Brown's old club, Burnley. The first of these games featured the début of a young Irish centre-half bought for £18,000 from Millwall. Not only did Charlie Hurley fail to stop the rot, he even assisted it by putting the ball through his own goal.

By the end of the first week in March Sunderland had gone 11 games without a win, and seemed certainties for the drop. Then came a brief revival: a run of two wins and three draws that lifted the club off the bottom and raised hopes.

Then, on 4 April 1958, Sunderland visited Old Trafford. As the club was finally relegated only on goal average (the worst goal average in Division One), it is possible retrospectively to look at any number of draws and defeats and hold them responsible. But the Manchester United away match was particularly galling. This was because Sunderland were on the end of their best spell of the season; because they had crept towards safety; and because goals from Revie and O'Neill gave them a 2–1 lead until the dying minutes.

Fear then crept in. Sunderland massed themselves back in their own half, and began time-wasting. United and their big home support, who had previously not seemed too bothered by the prospect of defeat (they were comfortably in the top half of the table), not only sensed the possibility of a draw, but – annoyed by their visitors – began to seek it. And they equalised at the death.

It was a disastrous week. Twenty-four hours later Birmingham won 6–1 at Roker, and two days after that Manchester United visited, and won 2–1. But astonishingly, Sunderland hung on to the bitter end. Their last game of the season was away at Portsmouth. Sunderland had 30 points before that match. Leicester had 31, and their last game was away at Birmingham. If Leicester lost, and Sunderland won, Leicester would go down and Wearside would be saved . . . Sunderland won 2–0. But Leicester also won, by 1–0.

After 68 years and 57 seasons, Sunderland AFC were relegated from Division One. It had been an incredible run. Aston Villa and Blackburn had both given up their similar record of consistent football in the top flight 20 years earlier. English football's most enduring record, set by its most consistent league side, had finally fallen. Wearside was simply stunned. It would be four seasons before Alan Brown collected a squad strong and confident enough to mount a serious challenge for promotion back out of Division Two.

Don Revie, the captain around whom Brown had hoped to rebuild his team, quickly deserted the sinking ship, transferring to Leeds United after precisely nine second flight matches. Daniel, Bingham, Fleming and a handful of others all joined Shackleton and Revie in the missing persons column. By the end of 1958 only one player remained from the old Division One side, the remnants of the Bank of England club – and he was Stan Anderson, the local man who had cost the club just a ten pound signing-on fee.

Anderson was made captain. In the early winter of 1958 it seemed as though he had been put in charge of a side which might make the double drop, from First to Third Divisions, as Sunderland sat at the bottom of Division Two. But they rallied, held their place, and prepared for the long haul back. The turning point should have come in the close season of 1961. Instead, the events of that July turned into one of the greatest lost opportunities, one of the most poignant playing tragedies, one of the biggest what-might-have-beens in the entire story of English football.

In that 1961 summer, with the whole of north-eastern football in the doldrums (Newcastle and Middlesbrough had joined Sunderland in Division Two), Middlesbrough's dynamic young striker Brian Clough had decided to take a sea cruise. When his ship docked back at Southampton, Clough was surprised when a man whose face he vaguely knew called him from the other side of the barrier. This stranger then gave half-a-crown to the porter carrying Clough's luggage, lifted the cases onto a trolley, turned round and said: 'Will you sign for Sunderland?' It was Alan Brown.

'Yes,' said Clough.

'Fine,' replied Brown. 'I'll see you at Roker Park in a week's time.'

In the previous season Sunderland had finished sixth in Division Two. Their directors continued loudly to insist to the fans that they would do anything, spend anything, to regain that Division One place. Paying Middlesbrough £42,000 for the centre-forward who was worth about a goal a game (he had netted 204 times in 222 matches for Middlesbrough) was real evidence of that commitment.

Clough was impressed by Brown. 'It was Alan Brown who taught me about discipline,' he would write:

> The Sunderland manager's approach was a shock to my system. He stood as straight as a Buckingham Palace guardsman and when he delivered a bollocking – my God, did you know you had been bollocked!
>
> There were occasions when I was downright scared of the man. He detested shabby clothing and insisted his players always had a regular trim. There was never a sign of long hair at Roker Park . . .
>
> He ran Sunderland from top to bottom. I recognised that from the start. What he said mattered, and people responded. He was the *boss* in every sense of the word and I said to myself, even then, 'If I ever become a manager – this is the way the job should be done.'

In his first season of 1961–62, Clough almost did it for Brown. This deadly striker scored 29 times in 34 league games: Sunderland scored a total of 85 goals – and they missed promotion by one point.

In 1962–63 the club was ready. Clough failed to score in his first four matches, and then he and his team-mates took off. With Stan Anderson and the brilliant Charlie Hurley marshalling from the back, and with Clough banging in 24 goals in his next 20 league games, Sunderland looked First Division material once again. The crowds flooded back and Wearside once more echoed to the Roker roar.

Tragedy then struck twice, firstly on 26 December 1962.

Sunderland, on top of Division Two, were playing Bury before an expectant 42,000 Boxing Day crowd. It was a terrible afternoon – sleet slashed across the ground, there was ice underfoot, and it was bitterly cold. But all was festive at Roker Park until left-back Len Ashurst played the ball to Brian Clough.

'I sprinted across the heavy, muddy surface towards the ball, my eye on it the whole time. I was never to be distracted in circumstances like that,' Clough remembers. 'Suddenly it was as if someone had just turned out the light. The Bury goalkeeper Chris Harker had gone down for the ball, and his shoulder crunched into my right knee. I was slightly off-balance, with my head down . . . My head hit the ground, and for a second or two I didn't know a thing.'

It is part of Roker mythology that when Brian Clough came to on that awful afternoon, with what was to prove a career-ending injury, he nonetheless began to drag his wrecked and bleeding body across the muddy penalty area, like some First World War hero in No Man's Land, towards the loose ball. This caused the Bury centre-half, a tall chap named Bob Stokoe, to tell the referee: 'Come on, he's only codding.'

'Not this lad,' said the ref. 'He doesn't cod.'

Clough had blood running down his face, but that was not the final blow. His crucial ligament behind the knee had torn. Thirty years later it might have been at least partly repaired, as Paul Gascoigne's was patched up, but in 1962 it was a vicious injury.

Brian Clough's leg had just been taken out of plaster, five months later, when the second blow struck Sunderland. After a dreadful April the team had rallied once again, won three consecutive games, and went into the last game of the season as favourites for promotion. That game, on 18 May 1963, was at home to Chelsea. Sunderland were on 52 points, in second place. Chelsea, who had two games left, were in third with 48 points. A draw at Roker Park would have clinched it. The local newspapers were so convinced of promotion that the *Sunday Sun* had already prepared a special celebratory issue.

Tommy Harmer scored an easy goal to give Chelsea a 1–0 win. And in their next match the Londoners won again, pipping Sunderland to Division One on goal average. John Gibson would write:

> For me the fine borderline between success and failure was never more clearly defined as when the final whistle was blown that day. [Sunderland captain Stan] Anderson, his chin buried in his chest as despair overcame him, trudged off alone and in misery, while no more than half a dozen paces away from him the jubilant Tommy Docherty was hugging and kissing the players who had incredibly pulled Chelsea out of the wilderness and into the land of plenty.

As the 1963–64 season began, the question was: would it be third time lucky? Sunderland's two consecutive years finishing in third place had convinced both friends and enemies that they were the club in waiting; that they were ready for the return. But it quickly became clear that they would have to do it without Clough and without Stan Anderson. Clough would spend the whole season jogging up and down the Roker terracing – often with Alan Brown running beside him to offer moral support – in an effort to regain fitness.

Anderson played until the end of September, when he was replaced in the first team by Martin Harvey, a Northern Ireland international full-back who had come up through Sunderland Youth. Then, on the morning of 6 November 1963, the bombshell burst.

Newcastle United's director Wilf Taylor telephoned the press and announced a press conference at St James's Park early that same afternoon. The journalists arrived to find Taylor, Alan Brown and . . . Stan Anderson. The impossible had happened. Anderson, the living symbol of Sunderland's resistance, was being transferred to the arch-enemy for £19,000. 'Please handle this story carefully and not controversially,' pleaded Brown.

Fat chance. Anderson himself looked, thought one reporter, like 'a man facing the death sentence instead of a new career'.

'From the age of 15 to 29,' Anderson would say later, 'I had been at Sunderland, and if that doesn't make an imprint on a person's life nothing will. I think I could have walked blindfolded from my home to my peg in the dressing rooms. My sudden break with them left me bewildered and unhappy.'

In those 14 years Stan Anderson had made 447 appearances at full-back, and had scored 35 goals. It was, at the time, a club appearance record. He had a decent career at Newcastle, captaining their promotion side a year later. But by that time Sunderland had already gone up themselves and Anderson – the man who had done more than any other to regain that Division One place for Wearside, and undoubtedly the man to whom the club's prestige meant most – was not there to enjoy it.

Promoted they were though, and in that sense the board and Alan Brown could not be faulted. They had a new goalkeeper in Jim Montgomery, two settled full-backs in Len Ashurst and Martin Harvey (both Montgomery and Ashurst would eventually better Anderson's appearance record), a brilliant captain and centre-half in Charlie Hurley, and the forwards – even without Brian Clough – were banging in the goals.

In the end Sunderland clinched promotion at a canter. In March and April gates of 40,000-plus saw the team clinch a series of home victories that put the club on top of Division Two. They were beaten to the Second Division title by Leeds United, thanks to a falling-off towards the season's end, but in the end the club won promotion by five clear points.

And almost immediately, before his new Sunderland could kick a ball back in the First Division, Alan Brown resigned. Brian Clough was not the only footballer who was sad to see this self-described 'players' manager' go. 'I've never left a club,' Brown would boast, 'without some of the lads weeping.' He went to Sheffield Wednesday, another club in crisis following a huge bribery scandal, and two years later he took the Yorkshire club to

Wembley and a set of FA Cup runners-up medals.

Brown was not around to see it, but Brian Clough did get to kick a ball for Sunderland in Division One. Without a manager, after a bad start to the 1964–65 season, with 15-year-old Derek Forster (the First Division's youngest-ever goalkeeper) standing in between the posts for the injured Jimmy Montgomery, the trainer and the board decided four matches into the campaign to risk their star striker once again – after an absence from competitive football of almost two years. And Cloughie scored. All three of his last league games were at home, and all were score-draws. The middle match of the three was at home to Don Revie's Leeds United. 'I stuck the ball through Jack Charlton's legs and scored,' Cloughie would record, to help gain a 3–3 draw before almost 50,000 fans.

Then he was advised to quit for good – the consulting specialist had always been concerned that further damage to the knee could, in 1964, result in permanent disability. Brian Clough is right to be proud of his astonishing scoring record. For Sunderland he netted 63 goals in 74 games. Overall he had a career aggregate of 251 goals in 271 first-class matches. That was, and remains, simply sensational. Aside from anything else, they were the quickest 251 goals ever scored at this level of English football. And he was forced to retire at the age of 29. We can only guess what might have been.

As it was, Clough did not immediately leave Wearside. In November the club appointed George Hardwick as manager. 'Sunderland banked their insurance money,' said Clough of his forced retirement, 'settling with me for little more than £1,000 as I recall, but the new manager George Hardwick offered me something that was to be far more significant than cash. He gave me the chance to work with the youth players.' He found, instantly, that he could teach: 'I'd only been doing the job a matter of months when Hardwick made me youth team manager.'

Sadly, neither Hardwick nor Clough lasted the year. Sunderland finished 15th in the first season back in Division One, and Hardwick was replaced by Ian McColl. When Clough approached the new manager to ask to keep his job, McColl refused, saying: 'I don't think the directors will be too pleased if you stay here.'

So Cloughie left with a testimonial at Roker Park – 30,000 fans giving him £10,000. In the boardroom after that game the chairman of Hartlepool United offered him a job as manager. Clough accepted. The rest is history – lost history, to Sunderland. The striker who might have been became the manager who might have been. Heaven knows, in the following years, Sunderland could have used him. McColl lasted two years, during which time the club hovered dangerously around the relegation area. He was replaced in the close season of 1968 by Alan Brown, returning for a second spell. And Brown did it again.

During his absence Brown had joined the Moral Rearmament right-wing fundamentalist group. He certainly had not lost his capacity to inspire faith in others. As Brown's Sunderland sank inexorably back towards Division Two, one of his coaches, Ian MacFarlane, mounted a spirited defence of this curious manager.

'For strength of character and all-round knowledge of the game,' said MacFarlane, 'this man is the tops. You don't have to win cups and league titles to be a success . . . Sunderland would have been without hope if he hadn't come back.' All of that is debatable. In response, most fans would have uttered just two words: Colin Suggett.

Sunderland had not enjoyed many successes during their time back in Division One. But Colin Suggett was certainly one of them. Signed on schoolboy terms from Chester-le-Street Boys back in 1964, after he had won the English Schools trophy and appeared for England Boys, Suggett captained Sunderland Youth to the FA Youth Cup in 1967, and appeared for the first team that same year.

This youngster from Washington, with the characteristic floppy hair, came as close to a local hero as the Sunderland fans allowed in the second half of the 1960s. Most satisfactorily, he was especially effective against Newcastle. In December 1967 Suggett grabbed two goals in four minutes against the Geordies to turn a game around that looked to be heading for defeat. In the following season Newcastle outplayed Sunderland at home and away, but on both occasions a single goal from the 20-year-old inside forward was enough to steal a 1–1 draw. Then Brown sold him. Sunderland had scored only 43 league goals in 1968–69 and Suggett had collected nine of them. The youngster clearly needed support. Instead, in June 1969 Alan Brown let him go to West Bromwich Albion for £100,000. It was a kind of record – he was the first north-easterner to command such a price.

The board had already spent most of the money on Calvin Palmer, a one-season wonder picked up from Stoke City for £70,000. Brown would complete the waste of £100,000 by paying £30,000 for the England striker Joe Baker. Neither of these much-heralded players did anything to save Sunderland from relegation. Neither of them looked for one moment like being an adequate replacement for the lost Colin Suggett.

Sunderland were relegated miserably in 1970. They won only six games in the whole season. 'We have already laid the foundations for a successful team,' said Alan Brown. 'Relegation is merely a temporary set-back.' In a curious sort of way, he was proved right. An extraordinary vindication was on the horizon. But Alan Brown would not be at the helm when it happened. At the end of October 1972 Brown was – for the first time in his managerial career – sacked. He was replaced by that former Bury centre-half who had been present at Brian Clough's injury, Bob Stokoe.

NINE

Into the Light

1973–2000

The arrival of Bob Stokoe at Roker Park marked the end of the long march of the history of Sunderland AFC, the end of the club's first hundred years. It marked the beginning of the modern era, an era which was characterised more than anything by a steady haul back to the very top level of English football; to the playing and spectating surroundings; and to a competitive environment which matched a club which, for half a century, had been the most consistently successful in the British game. And a slow haul it was, with many a step back along the way. For a few short months, however, it seemed that the ride might be quick and easy, because Bob Stokoe's first season turned out to be – there are no other words for it – sensational at the time, and in retrospect simply legendary.

Stokoe, who was born at Mickley, near Ripon in North Yorkshire, had progressed to become manager of Bury after their relegation to Division Three. He had then moved on to Blackpool. Despite all the talk from Alan Brown and his (dwindling) supporters about the strength of the squad which he had supposedly assembled – its Burnley-style youth policy and its tremendous potential – Stokoe did not inherit the most promising of units at Roker Park.

Suggett had not been the only promising young north-easterner to leave the club during Brown's second spell. A magnificent midfielder named Colin Todd had signed professional forms from Chester-le-Street Boys back in 1965 and had made the right-hand side of Sunderland's midfield his own since the beginning of the 1967–68 season. Brown had made Todd Sunderland captain at the age of 21, saying: 'We have not seen the best of Colin yet. He is improving all the time and I am sure that one day he will become the greatest player in England.' England manager Alf Ramsey agreed, picking Todd firstly for the national under-23s and then for the full England senior side.

And on 18 February 1971 this magnificent footballer, easily the best midfielder of his age in Britain, had been sold by Alan Brown for £175,000. He was bought by the manager of Derby County, a club which was enjoying a golden age under its abrasive young manager. That manager had, six years earlier, worked with the teenaged Colin Todd in the Sunderland youth team. His name was Brian Clough.

The great Charlie Hurley had also gone. Of all the players who stuck with Sunderland throughout the depressed years of the 1960s, Hurley was easily the most outstanding. His 400 appearances over 12 seasons had finally come to an end in the summer of 1969, when the brilliant Irish international was granted a free transfer to Bolton. Hurley would be rated by many fans as the greatest player ever to wear a Sunderland shirt. It was surely one of the saddest ironies of soccer that such a talent and such loyalty was rewarded by no major trophy, only the undying respect and devotion of Wearside.

Other experienced men like George Mulhall and Ralph Brand had also disappeared on a 'free', when their presence would have been most valuable to the local youngsters who – with Todd and Suggett – Sunderland had been bringing along. There was Mick McGiven, a teenaged half-back from Kenton who had been snatched from Newcastle Boys. But he had difficulty in settling in Sunderland's worried late-60s squad and was unfortunately booked three times and given a suspended suspension in his first senior season.

More happily, Richie Pitt from Ryhope, an England Schoolboys centre-half, seemed determined to do justice to Charlie Hurley's number five shirt – although such a baptism as his, at the age of only 17, could have broken a lesser footballer. All of the lad's first four games, in the spring of 1968, had been lost. Charlie Hurley's place would only finally be filled by the use of money – a lot of money, £100,000 which had been given to Rotherham United for the daunting figure of Dave Watson.

At the other end of the field, Denis Tueart had been another steal from Tyneside, picked up from Newcastle Juniors in 1967. Tueart was also inherited by Stokoe as a fully-fledged creative inside-forward or winger. He would in time – in not very much time – become a sensationally profitable transfer. When Tueart, who had cost precisely nothing, went, Sunderland would be a quarter of a million pounds better off. Alongside Tueart was the dynamic Scottish forward – again, already matured by the time of Stokoe's arrival – Bobby Kerr. And keeping both of them company in the forward line was another Scot whose game seemed to have just one small weakness. Ian Porterfield seemed a little shy in front of goal. He seemed to be lacking the killer touch.

But the most significant of them all was Jim Montgomery. This was the player who already had meant most of all to the club and the man who would become responsible for winning – as close to single-handedly as is ever possible in an 11-a-side team game – Sunderland's last and perhaps their most sensational major trophy. He was already 29 years old when Bob Stokoe arrived at Roker Park on 1 November 1972, already a record-breaking goalkeeper, and already spoken of as one of Sunderland's best-ever goalkeepers.

Montgomery, Wearside born and bred, had been signed from Sunderland Boys back in 1960. Sunderland almost missed this most inspirational of goalkeepers – he had spent a few weeks on trial at Burnley before being released and picked up by his local club. Following his début in February 1962, Montgomery became that most precious of assets: a fine goalkeeper who was utterly dependable, who took the position and made it his own, come hail or shine, come promotion or come relegation, season after season throughout the whole of the 1960s and into the 1970s. His only extended break from duty came in 1964 and 1965, when a pre-season training injury put him out of the side, to be replaced firstly by the 15-year-old Derek Forster, and then by the more threatening presence of Sandy McLaughlan. This accomplished Scot was bought from Kilmarnock for £12,000 and represented the only real opposition to Montgomery's extraordinary tenure between Sunderland's sticks in his record-breaking 15 years with the club. McLaughlan did not last. His bid to replace the local boy failed and he was sold back to Kilmarnock for just £2,500 after 46 games. Montgomery was back for good. The Sunderland board swallowed the financial loss on McLaughlan with relief.

He seemed never to grow old. Jimmy Montgomery was a youth when he first started to monopolise the Sunderland goalkeeper's shirt. He was still just a fresh-faced, beaming 29-year-old in the March of 1973, when chairman Keith Collings presented him with a gold watch on the occasion of his 457th game for the club – the match which broke Teddy Doig's 70-year-old appearance record. While still a young man – while still, in terms of some goalkeepers, a relative infant – Montgomery would go on to stretch that record surely beyond reclamation by any future challenger in twenty-first-century professional football. And no goalkeeper, surely, will ever in the future enjoy a cup final like Jimmy Montgomery's cup final.

Sunderland were already on their cup run when Montgomery received his gold watch. It came upon them – unusually – as an unexpected bonus. The team were sitting in the bottom half of Division Two when January came around in 1973. Thoughts of promotion had hardly crossed anybody's mind for several months; fears of relegation had been banished by Bob Stokoe getting the club on an instant winning streak; and as for the cup, well, a run would be nice. But as for winning it, that was out of the question. It was not just Sunderland and that old cup jinx. Second Division clubs did not win the FA Cup. The last Division Two side to win the cup had been West Bromwich Albion 42 years ago, back in 1931 – and they had done it in a promotion year. Everybody agreed that the top level of the game had got a lot sterner, a lot more ruthlessly efficient since 1931. There were teams about like Bill Shankly's Liverpool, Bertie Mee's Arsenal and Don Revie's Leeds. As a Second Division outfit you did not dare to dream of beating those guys in the FA Cup final. You had to join them first.

Sunderland never had made cup runs easy, and they were not about to set a precedent in 1973. The first three rounds, between the third and the fifth, took six matches – each one of them went to a replay. The third round should have been comparatively easy. Third Division Notts County were drawn away on 13 January 1973. County took the lead in Nottingham, and held that 1–0 advantage for most of the match. Then came a key moment; one which came close to exploding the whole dream at its start. With the seconds ticking away, Notts County's Les Bradd connected with a header and sent the ball hurtling towards Montgomery's top corner.

Jimmy Mongomery had many qualities as a goalkeeper. But perhaps the greatest of them was his reflexive ability. He was a magnificent strike saver. His reflexes were outstanding. Before very long the whole of Planet Football would become aware of that. At about 4.30 p.m. on 13 January 1973, some 15,000 people were made suddenly aware of it: the Sunderland keeper lunged for Bradd's header and saved it. Dave Watson then equalised. County travelled to Roker for the replay three days later – and Watson netted another one, as did Denis Tueart, to send Sunderland into the fourth round by 2–0.

At that stage, another Third Division club was rolled in. But there was a notable difference. This time it was Reading, this time the first game was at home – and this time the opposition's manager was the former Roker hero Charlie Hurley. Yet again it was a 1–1 draw, with the replay won 3–1 thanks partly to yet another cup goal from Dave Watson, picked at number nine to replace the injured Vic Halom.

By the time of the fifth round on 24 February 1973 there had been a cull of clubs from the upper reaches of Division One, and mid-table Manchester City had been installed as bookies' favourites for the trophy. Sunderland drew them away. Goals from Micky Horswill and Billy Hughes forced the draw at Maine Road. Billy Hughes collected two in a 3–1 win in the replay, but the inside-forward's brace was eclipsed by a once-in-a-lifetime thunderbolt from Vic Halom.

It may have been the next opposition which convinced sceptical Wearsiders that Sunderland were in with a shout at the FA Cup. They were, like Sunderland, a middling Second Division outfit. But Luton Town had traditionally held something of a hex over the men from Roker. Just a week before the quarter-final tie kicked off the Hatters had completed a league double over Stokoe's team. The 53,000 fans filed into the ground with some trepidation on 17 March, but they need not have worried. Luton hardly ever got out of their own half. Two defenders' goals, both in the second half, from Watson again and from left-back Ron Guthrie, put Sunderland in the semi-finals for the first time since 1956.

Of the four semi-finalists in 1973, three were formidable (two were reckoned to be irresistible forces) and the fourth – Sunderland – were assumed outside County Durham to be simply making up the numbers. The other three were Wolverhampton Wanderers (whose championship challenge had only just faded), Arsenal and Leeds United (both of whom still considered themselves to be in with a chance of a league and cup double).

The Arsenal and Leeds United teams of the early 1970s held English football to ransom. They were terrible twins. The styles evolved by their managers, Mee and Revie, were uncannily alike. They lived in fear of defeat. They were physically and mentally ugly teams, each the club hangover of Alf Ramsey's turgid World Cup-winning philosophy. They put a clamp on competition; held each match in an armlock. Outside Highbury and Elland Road they were universally feared and disliked.

And they were uncommonly successful. In 1971 Arsenal had

completed only the second twentieth century double. In 1972 they had contested the Cup final between them, and had been pipped to the championship only by Brian Clough's upstarts at Derby County. In the spring of 1973 Bill Shankly's Liverpool were thankfully providing some alternative competition at the top of Division One, but the turgid twosome progressed without much threat to the semi-finals of the cup.

The draw kept them apart. On 7 April Sunderland were matched with Arsenal and Leeds United were dancing with Wolves. If Sunderland were to win the FA Cup in 1973, they would have to shift an immoveable object and then oppose an irresistible force. It was probably impossible for any Second Division club – for any *English* club – to beat Arsenal and then Leeds in the FA Cup. Shankly's Liverpoool might just have scraped past them both, on a good day with a following wind. But not one journalist, not one fan, not one football insider beyond the north-east of England gave Sunderland a chance.

They took Arsenal first, in that semi-final at Hillsborough before 55,000 and the television cameras. With Manchester City gone, the London club had been installed as firm cup favourites. In an astonishing display of adventurous football, Sunderland took them apart. Vic Halom swooped to exploit a mix-up in the Arsenal defence, and then Billy Hughes made it 2–0. A late goal back from Charlie George failed to alter the result. Arsenal were out of the FA Cup by 1–2 to their old rivals. It was in itself a magnificent result and was applauded the length of the land. It also had reverberations. In beating Arsenal, Sunderland had opened a crack in the citadel walls. The most famous of all Arsenal supporters, Nick Hornby, remembers that game well. It signalled the end of a particular Arsenal regime. That inspired victory for Sunderland over Arsenal, wrote Hornby in *Fever Pitch*, 'prompted Bertie Mee to break the whole team up, but he never got a new one together again, and three years later he was gone . . . We could and should have won [the semi-final, and] the modern history of the club might have been entirely different.'

Not just the modern history of Arsenal, but of English football. Sunderland AFC are owed a big vote of thanks for jamming a spanner in Bertie Mee's works.

Next came Leeds United, Don Revie's Leeds United, at Wembley on 5 May 1973. If anything, Leeds in the final were judged to be a stiffer test than Arsenal in the semi-final. They had duly replaced Manchester City and Arsenal at the top of the bookies' list of odds. Leeds were harder, nastier, more skilful (when they allowed it to show) and hungrier. They had a kind of chippy greed for success, stemming from the brooding sense that Elland Road was somehow the land of the underdog itself, an unfashionable backwater nurturing a guerrilla campaign against everybody else. The fact that they were one of the great establishment clubs by 1973, being current FA Cup holders and having won the title just four years earlier, was not allowed to tarnish this useful self-image.

What, by contrast, did Sunderland have to offer this Wembley final? An honest, attractive, well-balanced team, beautifully motivated by the sergeant-major figure of Bob Stokoe; and a magnificent support which made the grand old stadium a humming bowl of red and white, and brought the occasion to life.

This was one of the finest of FA Cup finals. Stokoe led his men out in a tracksuit – and that set the tone. It quickly became clear that Stokoe expected his men to work for him, that he was there with them, a 12th man on the touchline – and that they were prepared to respond. The faces of the two sides told its story as they walked onto the pitch. Leeds were pinched, sour, hungry. Sunderland's representatives waved to the transplanted town on the terraces, smiled at each other, and got on with the job.

Ian Porterfield's goal came after half an hour. Billy Hughes hit a corner towards the menacing figure of Dave Watson at the back post. Watson and the ball missed each other – but Vic Halom stepped in, chested it down, and Porterfield whipped it high into the roof of the net.

The goal came too early for Sunderland's taste. Leeds had almost an hour in which to recover their rhythm; and recover it they did.

But Montgomery, Malone, Watson, Pitt, Guthrie and Horswill, aided tirelessly by Bobby Kerr, held out. The defining moment came half-way through the second half. A deep Leeds cross was met in mid-air by Trevor Cherry. His diving header was somehow kept out by Montgomery. That would in itself have been the save of the match. But Montgomery at full stretch could only lay the ball at the feet of Peter Lorimer.

Did the Scottish international have too much time? Did he overestimate the opportunity? Lorimer placed the loose ball neatly towards the open goal. He had not counted for Jimmy Montgomery's determination — or for the astonishing speed of the Sunderland keeper's reflexes. Montgomery scrambled back across his goal-line, whipped out an arm, and pushed the ball onto the crossbar. It rebounded to Malone, who cleared it — but nobody saw that. Sunderland and Leeds supporters alike were still watching the back of the net, where the ball should have been, or rubbing their eyes in disbelief. On radio and television, the live commentators were announcing a goal. A goal that never was . . . Lorimer slumped to the ground, made suddenly legless by astonishment. Montgomery urged his team-mates on.

The final immortal image came with the referee's whistle for the end of the match. Bob Stokoe, wearing a trilby and with his macintosh flapping over his tracksuit, ran onto the pitch and straight up to one player. Never had an FA Cup final been so comprehensively won — not saved, or strongly influenced, but actually decided — as was the 1973 final by Jimmy Montgomery.

And then there was the return to Sunderland: the 500,000 people stretched along the route to Roker Park; the great days of the middle of the 1930s revived; tales told by grandfathers brought back to life. Happy days were here again.

Bob Stokoe took Sunderland AFC back into Division One in the season of 1975–76, back as Division Two champions. But then ill-health and a poor string of results early in the season led this fine, honourable and inspirational manager to resign. For all his success, Bob Stokoe would never see his team win a game in the top flight.

The term 'managerial merry-go-round' is possibly over-used, even in the contemporary game, where the career expectancy of managers at some clubs is equivalent in duration to that of a First World War front-line officer. But no other term can be used to describe the extraordinary scenes at Roker Park for the next 19 years. The astounding statistics tell their own story. In those 19 seasons between the departure of Bob Stokoe in 1976 and the arrival of Peter Reid in 1995, Sunderland worked their way through no fewer than 17 managers (including Stokoe himself, returning for a brief second bite in 1986). Until Reid, only Denis Smith was around for three seasons or more – and he enjoyed a typically turbulent passage, lifting the club from the Third to the First Division, before dropping back down a snake to the Second once again.

The fall into Division Three was the turning point. In the new world of English professional soccer, the game was being rapidly divided into those who sank and those who swam. And the floaters were to be found in the top division of the league structure.

When Sunderland AFC first came to life, and for three-quarters of a century after that, the league was neither the most popular nor the most profitable competition. That distinction belonged to the FA Cup, the oldest and most prestigious club football trophy in the world. When Sunderland were sweeping all before them in the successful league campaigns of the 1890s and 1912–13, and 1935–36, fewer people would pay to watch the most important of league matches than would pack the ground to see an ordinary early-round cup-tie.

In the 1980s and the 1990s that all changed. The money required to sustain a club at the highest level could only be found in a regular and consistent league programme in what would become known as the Premiership. The FA Cup itself was supplanted not only in terms of prestige, but also in earning power, by the European Cup – access to which was, of course, determined by league performance. Clubs faced either the vicious circle of being outside the Premiership, therefore not earning the money needed to get into and stay inside the top division – or its happy counterpart, the virtuous circle of being in the Premiership and consequently generating the income necessary to stay there.

The final paragraphs of the distinguished history of Sunderland Football Club are therefore dominated by the club's utterly essential, life-and-death struggle to lodge itself among the winners in the twenty-first-century game.

That has been a battle so momentous that it eclipses yet another extraordinary achievement – that of Sunderland as yet again a Second Division club reaching the FA Cup final in 1992. The fact that Malcolm Crosby, with a side largely inherited from Denis Smith, should have made that long charge, speaks volumes for the indefinable spirit of Sunderland.

In the same year that John Byrne's seven goals (at least one against every cup opponent up to but sadly excluding the final, which was lost 2–0 to Liverpool) were taking Sunderland through to the club's fifth FA Cup final, another set of figures was forcing more unpleasant consequences. In 1992 the capacity of the Roker Park ground was reduced to 29,000. Over the following couple of seasons the stadium was further contracted, coming down to a capacity of just 22,657.

For the great old ground of a great old club in one of Britain's foremost footballing cities, this was unacceptable. It also had dire implications. No football club could realistically hope to sustain life at the top of the new English Premiership on 22,000 paying customers.

That is why the Stadium of Light at Wearmouth was proposed, funded, built and opened. It was far from being an untroubled move. Luckily, the right manager was found. This was by no means a certainty. The late-twentieth-century history of Sunderland is similar to that of several of its north-eastern neighbours in at least one regard. Their directors have always enjoyed an uncanny knack for picking the wrong manager.

Peter Reid was something of a gamble. A distinguished midfielder in his day, he had in 1994 been sacked by Manchester

City from his first managerial job. But towards the end of the 1994–95 season Sunderland were truly desperate. Another collapse into the third tier of English football seemed more likely than not. Vice-chairman Graham Wood accepted the provisional resignation of Mick Buxton and then met with Peter Reid.

Only seven matches were left to keep Sunderland in the First Division, and as Wood said: 'We were past the transfer deadline so there was nothing more we could do on the playing side. The only thing we could do was on the managerial side and history has proved that often does the trick.'

Reid seemed confident enough. He pleaded with the fans to play their part, and said that survival was possible. He agreed to take on the club for the remainder of the season, and to review matters after that.

It was tight, as tight as ever it had been. Reid's Sunderland got off to a perfect start. They won the first two of those crucial seven matches, both by 1–0, at home to promotion-chasing Sheffield United and away to Derby County. But after Luton had managed a 1–1 draw at Roker, the pressure was back on. Reid liked certainties, he said, 'cast-iron certainties', and the visit of Swindon Town to Sunderland on 22 April 1995 provided one. This was a classic six-pointer. Whoever won it was likely to stay up. Whoever lost it . . .

Martin Smith grabbed the only goal of the game. Two draws followed and Peter Reid had pulled his new club back from the brink.

He then went one better. Sunderland made a slow start to the 1995–96 season. After four games they were in the bottom half of the table. By New Year the club had risen to the edges of the play-off positions. But Reid's insistence that his Sunderland team was better than any other in the division was not yet transferred to reality. In fact, the manager's timing was perfect. As the days started to lengthen, so Sunderland's haul of points increased. Their early 1996 promotion push was distracted in the best possible way, by a dramatic two-game FA Cup tie against Manchester United. The Wearsiders were unlucky not to win the first game at Old Trafford, and went out by a single goal ten days later in the north-east. Bruised but not disconsolate, Reid's side got back to the bread-and-butter matter of gaining promotion.

By the end of February Sunderland had crept up to second place. But they were still five points adrift of leaders Derby County. That all changed with a 3–0 win over Derby which had Reid celebrating 'the best since I came here'. However, the manager still rated Derby as the best side in Division One. That also would change. Sunderland won at Birmingham; were duly applauded as certainties for promotion by the midlanders' manager Barry Fry; and went top of the table when the news came in that Derby had drawn at Watford.

And there they stayed, increasing their lead until they took the title and the automatic promotion place by four clear points. Roker was back on top.

It was the intention of all concerned that Sunderland's entry into the Premiership would coincide not only with the opening of this magnificent new home, but also with the progress of a side which was capable of staying there. Another hiccup, another slide back down, was not anticipated, but it came, and the Stadium of Light discovered itself a Second Division ground.

Not for long. Perhaps the most important, and certainly the wisest, decision taken by the Sunderland board at that point was the retention of Reid himself. It is due to this that Sunderland Association Football Club, secure in the hands of a talented and dedicated manager, were able to stroll back in the right direction in the last season of the twenieth century, losing just three league games all season and amassing 105 points – 18 more than second-placed Bradford City.

One hundred years before, Sunderland had been anticipating another new century. In 1899 the club looked back on a decade of unrivalled success, both on the field and off it. They had also just moved into the most sophisticated sports stadium in the north-east of England. They did not know it at the time, but those factors would combine for more than 50 years to produce a football club so memorable that the noise made by its fans became a national by-word. Following the fortunes of Sunderland Association Football Club through those decades gave everything that the game has to offer – elation, despair and a minimum of mediocrity. Whatever Sunderland have done, they have done it with style and commitment. When they spent, they spent big; when they erred, they erred drastically; but when they entertain they do so in the grand, lavish manner. Lucky those who will be present in the new millennium to see the club stride into the light.

Sunderland AFC Chronology

1879	Sunderland & District Teachers' Association Football Club formed.
1881	Sunderland Association Football Club formed.
1890	Elected to twelve-team, one division, three-year-old Football League.
1890–91	First season in Football League, finished 7th; beaten semi-finalists in FA Cup.
1891–92	League champions; beaten semi-finalists in FA Cup.
1892–93	League champions.
1893–94	League runners-up.
1894–95	League champions; beaten semi-finalists in FA Cup.
1896–97	Finish second-bottom of Division 1, narrowly escape relegation in play-offs.
1897–98	League runners-up.
1900–01	League runners-up.
1901–02	League champions.
1912–13	League champions, beaten Cup finalists.
1922–23	League runners-up.
1934–35	League runners-up.
1935–36	League champions.
1937	FA Cup winners.
1957–58	Relegated from Division One.

1963–64	Promoted from Division Two.
1969–70	Relegated from Division One.
1973	FA Cup winners.
1975–76	Promoted from Division Two as champions.
1976–77	Relegated from Division One.
1979–80	Promoted from Division Two.
1984–85	Relegated from Division One.
1986–87	Relegated from Division Two.
1987–88	Promoted from Division Three as champions.
1989–90	Promoted from Division Two.
1990–91	Relegated from Division One.
1995–96	Promoted from Division One as champions to Premiership.
1997–98	Relegated from Premiership.
1998–99	Promoted from Division One as champions.